DEMONS AND
SPIRITS OF THE LAND

"What are the ancient mysteries of earth and water? Guided by the sure hand of Claude Lecouteux in this erudite and accessible book, we find keys to the recovery and renewed understanding of indigenous European religious traditions concerning land and water. A valuable book—highly recommended."

ARTHUR VERSLUIS, AUTHOR OF
SACRED EARTH AND *RELIGION OF LIGHT*

"*Demons and Spirits of the Land* is a scholarly investigation of the spirits present in the traditional landscape of Europe. Claude Lecouteux explains how humans are inseparable from our surroundings: we are not the only intelligent beings, for we cohabit the Earth with other sentient entities. Traditionally, these entities manifest as land spirits who take many forms: giants, dwarves, brownies, fairies, and dragons. Present in the land, they must be dealt with if humans are to live in harmony and well-being. This book details rites and ceremonies of coming to terms with the spirits of tree and forest, spring and mountain, taken from comprehensive documentary and folklore sources, including ancient authors, Arthurian legends, medieval romances, and Norse sagas. If you want to know about the nature of land spirits and how we relate to them, this is essential reading."

NIGEL PENNICK, AUTHOR OF
THE BOOK OF PRIMAL SIGNS: THE HIGH MAGIC OF SYMBOLS

"A superbly written treatise on the folklore of place, showing how the church has demonized once revered and respected land spirits. The setting up of high crosses, statues of saints, and the ringing of bells has been done for two thousand years to repel and control the fairies, elves, dragons, dwarves, and giants our ancestors once placated and venerated. But are we better off for all the church's civilizing efforts?

"We are now at a turning point in human history where we need to come to terms with what we have wrought. The Earth Mother has given us food, healing, and shelter, and we have abused her in return. Reading these pages we learn that the dark path through the wilderness may once again lead us to a sacred space within the forest where in respectful company with the ancient deities, land wight's, and the fey, we may yet resume our ancient offerings, begin the healing, and return to harmony with all creation."

DEMONS AND SPIRITS OF THE LAND

Ancestral Lore and Practices

CLAUDE LECOUTEUX

Translated by Jon E. Graham

Inner Traditions

Rochester, Vermont • Toronto, Canada

Inner Traditions
One Park Street
Rochester, Vermont 05767
www.InnerTraditions.com

Text stock is SFI certified

Originally published in French under the title *Démons et Génies du terroir au Moyen Âge* by
    Éditions Imago
First U.S. edition published in 2015 by Inner Traditions

Library of Congress Cataloging-in-Publication Data
Lecouteux, Claude.
    [Démons et Génies du terroir au Moyen Age. English]
    Demons and spirits of the land : ancestral lore and practices / Claude Lecouteux ;
foreword by Régis Boyer ; translated by Jon E. Graham. — First U.S. edition.
        pages cm
    "Originally published in French under the title Démons et Génies du terroir au Moyen
Age by Éditions Imago."
    Includes bibliographical references and index.
    ISBN 978-1-62055-399-2 (pbk.) — ISBN 978-1-62055-400-5 (e-book)
    1. Demonology. 2. Demonology—History of doctrines—Middle Ages,
600–1500. I. Graham, Jon E., translator. II. Title.
    BF1511.L4313 2015
    133.4'20940902—dc23
                                                                    2014045511

Printed and bound in the United States by Lake Book Manufacturing, Inc.
The text stock is SFI certified. The Sustainable Forestry Initiative® program promotes
sustainable forest management.

10 9 8 7 6 5 4 3 2 1

Text design and layout by Debbie Glogover
This book was typeset in Garamond Premier Pro with Gill Sans MT Pro and Oriya MN as
display fonts

Inner Traditions wishes to express its appreciation for assistance given by the government
of France through the National Book Office of the Ministère de la Culture in the
preparation of this translation.

*Nous tenons à exprimer nos plus vifs remerciements au gouvernement de la France et au
ministère de la Culture, Centre National du Livre, pour leur concours dans la préparation de
la traduction de cet ouvrage.*

Contents

PART THREE

Survivals and Transformations

Foreword

It has become a routine: a new book by Claude Lecouteux appears on what is conveniently (and mistakenly, I might add) called "lower" mythology; the unexpected juxtaposition of cultures we do not customarily associate with one another produces totally surprising conclusions; and from this we conclude that we should definitely revise our habits and ways of looking at such subjects. Over the last few years (for Claude Lecouteux shows a rare prolificacy) we have seen this process occur with regard to ghosts and revenants, then elves and dwarves, and finally witches, werewolves, and fairies—in short, all those more or less tenebrous inhabitants that dwell in the back regions of our collective unconscious and which we are incapable of expelling from our representations or easily incorporating into our "religious" world.

And this is because such entities do fall into the religious category; there can be no doubt about that. Although their contours may have deteriorated over time, they assume a status like that of gods and their history is as worthy as that of the greatest myths; the worship we pay them, in whatever form, fits right in with all of the classical religious pomp and circumstance. They have only been victims of a devaluation, largely brought about by the Church, but they remain vitally alive despite our lack of awareness, or they continue on in all kinds of disguises that we do not necessarily recognize. And Claude Lecouteux, with the methodical rigor that makes his work so important, investigates, compares, contrasts, and confronts them. He has the gift of being able to leap from one culture to another with a casualness, a virtuosity, and, on reflection, a pertinence that renews our perspectives and opens up entirely new paths. Yes, he is a scholar of medieval Germany, but he also has a weakness for ancient Scandinavia, which is a good thing. The varied accounts that he writes about derive from myriad sources, and the comparisons he makes are almost always compelling. Someday I would really like him to have done with all these juxtapositions and confrontations, and to reveal his ulterior motives. Just where is he heading, strolling like this from culture to culture by virtue of a particular theme? What possible outcome could there be for this vast and remarkably documented investigation? Clearly, something persists in all these transformations that a god, a sacred concept, a myth, or a rite can undergo. Obviously this "hard core" comes from a spirit and essence that is deeper than all the superficial fantasies inscribed in our texts. This is what we need to learn how to read.

In principle, there is no reason to reject Claude Lecouteux's intuitions nor the approach that he takes. The following postulate is implicit: the *homo religiosus* inside all of us has always lived in a dual and therefore haunted world. The supernatural, the marvelous, and the fantastic comprise an aspect of our universe, and we exert considerable effort at recreating, rediscovering, taming, and exorcising this aspect. (There is no reason to be miserly when it comes to finding verbs for identifying the variety of our reactions.) Before the time when reason got the upper hand, there was an age when the anthropomorphizations and individuations took place that were responsible for the emergence of our gods and their organization into pantheons. The idea of the divine (the immortal, the timeless, the perfect, the necessarily unique, and so forth—there is no end to these characterizations!) did emerge, in fact had to emerge, from such processes as anthropomorphization and individuation—either one or the other, or indeed both, for they are not contradictory.

We can, in fact, trace the very idea of divinity back to the great natural forces, the primordial, fundamental elements of our world that define us as much as they frighten us: water, sun, fire, earth—especially the earth, as we shall see—and their emanations, if I may refer to them in this way: wind, thunder, and so on. Among the ancient Scandinavians, a world closer to our origins than other more "time-worn" cultures, there are plenty of divine entities for literally expressing all these components (to give just one example, Thor has a name that literally means "thunder"). But we might prefer going back to the great ancestors, the founders of all our lineages, the sovereign dead responsible—it goes without saying—for our current existence. I don't mean to imply that they are all keepers of great sacred secrets, though they have crossed the boundary and allegedly know what we expend such great effort to learn our whole life. I am only trying to emphasize the fact that they have undoubtedly "gone back to the land" and are now a part of its very substance: "*homo-humus*," as Mircea Eliade liked to say, which is in no way contradicted by the fine old myth of Adam's birth "from the dust of the ground" (Genesis 2:7).

So whether the origins come from a state of things; or because the Earth as such (which I will refer to as "she" because she is obviously the support of all fertility and I have always considered that to be the most fundamental value of Dumézil's system) has always been our greatest and only deity, Terra Mater, the likely expression of all the Great Goddesses or Earth Mothers of our various religions; or the origins go back to a stage when this Earth was viewed as the accumulation of the substance of the great ancestors, it seems hard to deny that she must have been our first sacred entity. She may have been replaced by the sun (the sun is feminine in the majority of archaic religions) or water, but that does not alter things to any meaningful extent. In any event, what emerges as an expression of our religious awareness is a supernaturalized natural universe.

Beyond any shadow of a doubt, this is the reason that we have always lived in a haunted universe. After studying monsters, giants, dwarves, and other happily indistinguishable inhabitants of the collective mind, it is easy to see why Claude Lecouteux would go back to the source in order to grapple with the heart of the matter. What we might customarily term a *genius loci,* he chooses to call a "land spirit." A wise choice. The investigation he conducts is decisive: we evolve within an inhabited "natural" world; one in which the gods themselves, or the deified dead, or just simply the dead, are the cornerstone of reality. As a result, it is a world that cannot conform to appearances. The ground we walk on is hollow, the water of the spring is too well demarcated to be innocent, the forest houses monsters, and the mountain or moor has a soul.

This definitely explains a number of the gestures, quasi rites, and outright rituals that are described for us by the ancient texts, as well as those things we call folklore and those that fall into the corpus of our age-old superstitions—which are still very much alive! The Old Icelandic *Landnámabók* (Book of Settlements) and some sagas are quite explicit on this point, but there is no culture that does not dwell upon this subject in one way or another. The Balts and the Slavs, for example, whom Claude Lecouteux only deals with peripherally, would supply him with a rich harvest of details concerning their tutelary spirits and the way they transform the scenery of our lives into a kind of palimpsest. And even in Iceland, the *Eyrbyggja saga* describes a scree called Geirvor that contains a talking head, which at one point delivers an ominous poetic verse. Is there any better way to sense the continuity between irregularities in the landscape and the most exalted human activities? Claude Lecouteux speaks of the "underside of idolatry" and the "evidence of place-names" (he could easily have reversed the two descriptions), and it leads me to declare that nothing is innocent in our world. It is not the "sleep of reason" that produces monsters—to the contrary, there are monsters everywhere that the sacred manifests itself, and we have no choice but to partially suspend our reason in order to admit this fact and take consequent action.

Claude Lecouteux's successive studies have confined themselves definitively and deliberately within a powerful tautology. He started with monsters (fairies, witches, and werewolves) and now he is introducing us to the land spirits. He has wisely charged the "small" deities (a much better choice than the "great" gods) with the task of educating us about the actual content of our condition.

There are two things that have always struck me about the research that he has pursued so conscientiously. The first is that I can momentarily catch sight of his absolute rejection of realism, positivism, scientism, and all those *isms* that deny the "profound" aspect (as Nietzsche called it) of our world. Out of a conviction that feels solidly anchored, and employs the most proven scholarly methods, he allows us to see that we live in a dual world, endowed with a living soul. A sacred world. If religion is the art of "binding" (as one etymology for the word would have have it, from Latin *re-ligere*) our material domain to another immaterial but equally effective one, then there is nothing more religious than an approach of this nature. It continually erects bridges between our doubts and anxieties (or our allegedly short-sighted ignorance) and this supremely vital immaterial realm—a realm that cannot be described as something of our own creation or the fruit of our imagination.

This is because—and here is the second thing—his research offers evidence of a Force, a Spirit of Force, a Spirit of Life-force, one that infinitely overwhelms us at the same time as it encompasses us. I am happy to learn that our environment is *animated*—this is exactly the right word—by these sacred emanations that, in the final analysis, amount to a life that is higher and more perfect than our own. All of these gestures described by Claude Lecouteux, these rites of circumambulation, for example, these reflexive acts of exorcism or propitiation, these votive attitudes, are manifestations of reverence toward Life—real Life that does not die and makes itself known under the guises of the imposing natural forces, and of course that Life to which our aforementioned great ancestors have testified better than any other.

In sum: it is a gesture of worship that Claude Lecouteux, perhaps unknowingly, invites us to make. There is a Life-force that stirs our hearts and minds everywhere, as it always has. It appears under a thousand different faces and in countless stories and cultic gestures, but it is never absent from our wanderings. We are literally bathed in its radiance. And some of its surest anchor-points are precisely those spots, those pieces of land, that speak to us through the intermediary of all these creatures that, in our thirst to justify the obvious, we have crafted but which all evidence indicates existed before all our efforts of interpretation—for they are theophanies or hierophanies.

RÉGIS BOYER,
LA VARENNE

Régis Boyer is professor emeritus of Scandinavian languages, literature, and civilization at the University of Paris–Sorbonne and director of the Institute of Scandinavian Studies. He is the author of numerous books, including *La Grande Déesse du Nord* (The Great Goddess of the North), *Le Monde du double: la magie chez les anciens Scandinaves* (The World of the Double: Magic among the Ancient Scandinavians), *La Poésie scaldique* (Skaldic Poetry), *Sagas légendaires islandaises* (Legendary Sagas of Iceland), and *Yggdrasill: la religion des anciens Scandinaves* (Yggdrasill: The Religion of the Ancient Scandinavians).

We Dwell in a Haunted Place

In the beginning there was space and the space was frightening. Man felt lost within it, confronted as he was by its vastness, a source of uncertainty and mystery. It took countless centuries for man to learn to know the earth, investing in it and mastering it. Subject to the whims of nature, washed by the rains and dried by the winds, warmed by the sun and chilled by the frosts, amazed or stricken by phenomena he was utterly incapable of grasping, man felt like an intruder inside a wild and still untamed nature, or at least this is how he perceived it. He then reacted with all the means at his disposal. He learned to know the plants and animals and assured his survival by giving them names. He deified all that threatened or awed him, and implemented propitiatory rites. In short, he developed a religious sensibility. Everywhere around him he saw traces of the invisible, traces of another reality attesting to the presence of myriad unspeakable creatures.

Without our knowing, we dwell in a haunted space—certainly more than in former times when the ghosts of vanished generations continued to accompany the living, when technological progress had not depopulated the spirit world. If you need convincing, simply cast a glance at the folk traditions that persisted into the dawn of the twentieth century in the rural areas across all Europe. One need only glance at any detailed map to find the Fairy Rocks, Devil's Bridges, the Pierrefittes,* and the Dragon Springs, and if we take the trouble to leaf through the delightful works of nineteenth-century regional scholars, we will discover that every forest has its spirits, every spring its lady, every river has malevolent beings in its depths, that dwarves dance on the moors, that the marshes are teeming with will o' the wisps—which, we are told, are lost souls—and that the mountains are home to demons and wild folk who enjoy causing landslides, avalanches, and floods.

Studying the relations that our remote ancestors maintained with their environment is one means of better understanding humanity, for we are inscribed within history like links of a chain, and if we want to understand our world and that of our ancestors, we have to look back.

The field of research upon which I am embarking here is already known to some experts who have clearly recognized that space is sacred, without, however, going beyond that observation. In France, the organization "Société de Mythologie Française" has often shown that the human being is inseparable from his natural surroundings and that his relationship with it structures his imagination, steers his thoughts, and incorporates him within the cosmos. The study of mythical geography— the legends, myths, and beliefs attached to places—has revealed the importance of the local landscape in the formation of tales and rites. Place-names, in combination with scriptural and epigraphic accounts, make it possible to discover the roots of beliefs, as the traces still survive almost everywhere and these place-names function as supports in the collective memory. Some components of the landscape have been the subject of monographs—mountains and forests, for example—but the most interesting considerations are to be found in articles from specialized journals that are little known to the general public, and in works dealing with completely different topics.

---

*[Pierrefittes is a recurring place-name in France that originally referred to megalithic monuments in the landscape. Much folklore surrounds such sites. —*Trans.*]

Medieval literature in Latin and in the vernacular languages offers the advantage of presenting us with real or fictionalized accounts from an era in which Cartesian rationalism and the so-called exact sciences had not yet elevated doubt and experimentation to the status of canonical virtues. The Arthurian romances depict a world in which everything is possible, with supernatural beings as well as God and the saints all making their appearances. The historical chronicles are filled with marvels and oddities, and the bestiaries are rich with inconceivable animals. By patiently collating these texts, shunning no written works, it is possible to draw up the little-known history of land spirits—those spirits that medieval Christians rejected as "demons."

But to what, exactly, does the term "land spirit" refer? The word "spirit" has various meanings; among other things, it designates a tutelary deity attached to an individual, or a supernatural being endowed with powers surpassing our understanding, and it is also a synonym for "demon, elf, fairy," and so on. In modern French, the land where this spirit dwells would be a *terroir,* a word that derives from the vulgar Latin *territorium,* originally designating a territory, a country, or an expanse of land; later, a soil good for the cultivation of wine; and lastly, a rural region. (The latter two senses are essentially the meaning of *terroir* as it survives today.) The term "land spirit" is my translation for the Latin *genius loci,* "place spirit"; in other words, a *numen,* a *daimon* attached to a specific place that it owns and protects against any incursion. By "place" I mean an uninhabited land that is still wild and uncultivated. Thus, I will not be dealing with household spirits, who are attached to a dwelling, because that subject is too large and deserves its own monograph to do justice to all its many facets. This distinction—which may seem arbitrary in light of the fact that land spirits can easily become domestic spirits—is therefore necessary, and it prevents us from going astray along the meandering paths of now almost completely erased ancestral traditions about which the texts speak little, as is the case with anything controversial.

The clerical interpretation of pagan beliefs and their demonization have, until now, formed an obstacle to the understanding of scriptural accounts as well as their interpretation. One question continually arises: are we dealing here with a spirit or a devil, a spirit or a demon? Another question accompanies this one: how truthful are the texts? Furthermore, is it really necessary to view the fictional literature as being in opposition to the scholarly or clerical texts, or the culture of the elite in opposition to the popular culture? I do not think so, because every narrative is fueled by reality and is its mirror. It can certainly be a distorted mirror, but it is a mirror nonetheless.

Are there one or more fundamental differences between the Roman, Celtic, and Germanic worlds? The reading of the texts obliges us to answer in the negative because the divergences are most often the result of local adaptations of identical structures: ecotypes, in other words. This all compels us to offer a postulate that there are many *anthropological structures of the imaginal realm*, as Gilbert Durand has shown, that show little variation, at least among the various Indo-European peoples. Of course they are all at a similar stage of development; that goes without saying. If there are any doubts, reread the great classic Frazer's *The Golden Bough,* or Krappe's *La Genèse des Mythes* (The Genesis of Myths), or a few books by Mircea Eliade. The examples given in these works are taken from all of the earth's peoples and the similarities are baffling. As a correlate of the postulate given above, I suggest that the imagination feeds on *realia*—transforming, transposing, and projecting them into the realm of myth, or maintaining them in the sphere of beliefs that are mistakenly labeled superstitions.

In the dossier I am presenting here, which is an extension of my research into the strange and unusual creatures from medieval literature—ghosts, revenants, dwarves, elves, fairies, witches, and werewolves—the crucial question remains the following: how do we identify a spirit beneath its various disguises?

The same problem arose for Pierre Saintyves when he studied the saints, behind whom were not only concealed the gods (his major theory) but also the spirits of the land. As it was reconstituted into literary forms and/or Christianized, the folk memory combined different individuals and regrouped them under generic names like dwarves and elves, giants and devils, and even dragons or fairies—who were not merely the direct heirs of the Parcae. The transposition of these beliefs into the domain of the marvelous allowed these beings to survive and weather the anathema of the ecclesiastical authorities, for whom such things were nothing but pagan remnants that needed to be eradicated—*delenda est superstitio!*

The spirits became perpetually mutating beings. Their shape, names, and appearances were protean, but their role, duties, and localization remained unchanged. In earlier studies I provided proof of this concerning elves and dwarves, whose connections with the world of the dead are striking. But it should be clearly noted that this is the characteristic of all extremely archaic creatures that are suggestive of primitive animism, which anthropomorphizes natural forces before they are eventually absorbed by the religions that form around them.

Narrative literature and the romances make use of this legacy. The more or less anthropomorphized spirits become human-like individuals, playing supporting or adversarial roles (as in the more recent tales), or they retain all their mystery (as in the story of Melusine). Who are these mysterious surveyors who emerge from nothingness to mark out the boundaries of the future domain of Lusignan? Those which have taken form as animals should not be excluded either, nor should inanimate forms, for in fact the spirit frequently evades any particualar shape. And if it sometimes resembles a human being, it is appropriate to ask ourselves whether this might not be a convention, a way to better grasp something that was ceaselessly escaping understanding. Look at what Paracelsus said about elementary spirits, and consider too the figure of Kühleborn (Fontfroide), the water spirit in Friedrich de la Motte-Fouqué's *Undine:* it can take on any appearance, that of a man or that of a jet of water.

Once we have put the civilized space behind us, we literally enter the other world: that of the land spirits who preside over the various domains and who are hidden everywhere. A very lively German legend tells how one of these beings became the spirit of a place. In order to build his farm, a peasant cut down some trees and the spirit entered the house when the beams were brought in. If it is treated well—meaning if it is shown respect and given offerings on specific dates—the spirit becomes a valuable assistant, but it can be mischievous at times and sow such disorder in the household that the inhabitants will try to get rid of it. As long as a farm possesses an even-tempered spirit, the estate will prosper. Here we have caught a glimpse of the origin of the household spirit.

We shall begin by diving into this mystery, collecting examples of odd facts that remain unexplained. To see only marvels or "great dev-iltries" here, as they said during the Middle Ages, is to remain on the surface of things, to content ourselves with literary labels—in other words, to tackle the problem solely from the angle of how it was recy-cled in fiction. Alas, this is an error that is still committed far too often. We shall then examine the problem of the peopling of the earth—who came before man? Finally, we shall deal with those fictional accounts that bear witness to what became of the land spirits.

PART ONE

A Haunted Universe

The land spirit often takes the form of a dragon.
Illustration from an early German edition of
The Travels of Sir John Mandeville.
Basel: Bernhard Richel, 1480–1481.

1
Unusual
Manifestations

During the Middle Ages, countless texts were literally teeming with fantastic passages, sometimes accompanied by an explanation but more often presented with impenetrable brevity. They implicitly refer to the existence of an occult world, the laws of which are also in force on this plane. Authors frequently extricated themselves from this situation by recasting the facts from a Christian perspective in which they could be viewed as manifestations of divine omnipotence, for God is admirable in all his acts and the human mind is incapable of penetrating His secrets.

In the *Konungs skuggsjá* (King's Mirror), written in Norway around 1260, there appears an Irish island that floated atop Lake Loghica. It only touched land on Sunday and healing herbs grew there. In the same book, we also find a particular spring whose water tastes like beer: "When men try to build a house over the spring, it moves and gushes outside the dwelling" (chap. 13). Further on, we see Lake Loghaerne (today called Lough Ree), which lies between the counties of Roscommon, Langford, and Westmeath in Ireland. The lake is covered with islands and on the largest of these, Kertinagh, the devils have as much power as they do in hell (chap. 14). According to other legends, the Purgatory of Saint Patrick is found on this island.

In his *Topographia Hibernica* (Topography of Ireland), Giraldus Cambrensis (Gerald of Wales, ca. 1146–1223) mentions a lake that extends north of Munster and has two islands. No one can die on the smaller of the two isles and it is therefore called the Island of the Living (*Insula viventium*).[1] In his *Itinerarium Cambriae* (Journey through Wales), this same Gerald describes a stone that returns to the spot from which it has been taken. Hugh, the Earl of Shrewsbury, had it chained in another location but his efforts were in vain: the stone returned to its original location.[2] A similar phenomenon can be seen in the *Historia Brittonum,* attributed to Nennius. The stones removed from the tumulus where King Arthur's dog Cabal is buried return of their own volition to the cairn (chap. 73). Nennius also talks of a mountain that revolves three times a year, stones that walk about at night, and a glass tower in the middle of the sea (chap. 75).[3]

The *Konungs skuggsjá* also recounts an interesting legend about Themar (Teamhar), better known today as Tara, the former capital of Ireland. The king rendered judgment there while seated on a throne placed upon a rise. One day he pronounced an iniquitous judgment and the earth turned upside down: "What had been below was now above, all the houses and the royal hall sank into the depths of the earth" (chap. 15). The *Liber Monstrorum* (Book of Monsters), written around the year 1000, states: "It is said that monsters with three human heads live in the marshes, and a fable relates that they live in the depths of ponds like nymphs."[4]

These simple examples show immediately that unknown forces exist that sometimes assume a shape, such as that of a human or animal, or even an inanimate object. These creatures or objects in fact embody the forces in question and are a more expressive way of representing the latter.

Gervase of Tilbury, who around 1210 wrote his *Otia Imperialia* (Recreation for an Emperor) dedicated to Emperor Otto IV of Brunswick, also reported strange things. He mentions the city of

Terdona in Italy, where "Every time the head of a family is destined to die in the coming year, blood flows in one of the furrows cut by a plough blade on his lands" (III, 7). In Catalonia, in the bishopric of Girona, there stands a mountain at the peak of which lies a lake of deep black waters whose depth cannot be sounded. "It is said this is the site for a dwelling of demons. . . . If a stone or something heavy is cast into the lake, a storm bursts out at once, as if the demons were angered" (III, 66).[5] In his thirteenth-century *Cronica* (Chronicle), Salimbene di Adam indicates that Peter III of Aragon was caught in a storm one day on Mount Canigou. He found a pond and threw a stone into it, whereupon a dragon emerged that soared over the waters.[6] Near Carlisle, in the British Isles, Gervase of Tilbury maintains there is a valley surrounded by mountains in the heart of a great forest where "Every day at a certain time, a melodious carillon of bells can be heard there" (III, 69). Why does this spring in the diocese of Uzès change location if something dirty is placed in it (III, 129)? Why do the coffins that float down the Rhône stop of their own accord at the Aliscamps cemetery (III, 90)? In the province of Aix, Gervase claims, there is "a huge cliff whose steep face is pierced with windows" in which appear "two or three ladies who appear to be conversing" but who vanish when approached (III, 43). In Livron Castle in the bishopric of Valence, there is a tower that cannot stand the presence of a night watchman: the man is carried away and deposited far down below in the valley (III, 20).[7]

Let us shift our focus to some other horizons. According to the *Guta saga* (Saga of the Gotlanders), which originally dates back to the early first half of the thirteenth century, the island of Gotland was enchanted (*elvist*) before it was colonized. During the day it sank beneath the waves and resurfaced at night.[8] This story cannot help but bring to mind that of Tintagel Castle. In the twelfth-century Oxford version of *La Folie Tristan* (The Madness of Tristan), it was called the enchanted castle (*chastel faez*), because it vanished twice a year:

Tintagel li chastel faez
Chastel fä fu dit a droit
Kar dous faiz le an se perdeit . . .
Une en ivern, autre en esté. *

We may also wonder about the meaning of the following facts: the Lake of Granlieu had the right of high, middle, and low justice. The tribunal sat in a boat two hundred feet from shore, and when the judge delivered a sentence, he had to touch the water with his foot.[9]

We quickly realize, on reading such narratives, that our world is haunted by invisible beings and forces, and this opinion persists into the present, which is proven time and again by the folk traditions and beliefs that have been collected up until the very recent past. Spirits loom up everywhere and place-names confirm the existence of mysterious figures, or at least the persistence of their memory. Here we have "Dragon Spring" (for example, the Foun del Drac in Lozère), and there the "Fairy Well" or the "Fountain of the Ladies," names that evoke the spirits that preside over springs. During the fifteenth century it was almost proverbial to say something was "as naked as a fairy coming out of the water."

Water, whether running or stagnant, reputedly sheltered many creatures, the majority of whom were dangerous. Mahwot from the Meuse River had the appearance of a lizard. Similar ones include the Vogeotte of the Doubs, the Carne Aquoire of the Blois region, the Drac of Auvergne, the Alsatian Hôgemann (the "Man with the Fang"), the "Havette Beast" of the region near the Hague, the Serpent of the Trou Baligan (Lower Normandy), the Gourgoule of the Underground Wells (Limousin), the Uillaout of Savoy, and the Morvandious Queular.[10]

Forests are home to will o' the wisps and to the Hannequets of

---

*Tintagel, the enchanted castle / the magic castle it is said in sooth / For it disappears twice a year / Once in winter, and again in summer.

the Argonne, the Breton Kornikaned (Korrigans), the "Weeper of the Woods" from the Pontarlier region, the Waldensian Hutzeran, and the Ardennes Bauieux, and the Bredoulain Woods is the lair of the Huyeux. In the Ain region we find the Sauvageons; in the Beaujolais, the Fayettes; and Green Ladies, giants, and sprites abound almost everywhere.

On the moors, wisps, dwarves, white ladies, night shepherds (*bugul-noz*), alarming crones (*groah*), and sprites (the *faulaux* in Lower Normandy) come out to dance and attend to their occupations.

The mountains are a veritable refuge of genies and spirits, devils and demons. Here swarm the Daruc, a kind of werewolf, Nuitons, and Naroves (Savoy),[11] the Gögwargi (Upper Valois), and fairies. More than one farm has its Servan, a kind of domestic spirit, and the *fouletot* of the Jura Alps steals, feeds, and returns the finest cow of the herd while the cowherd is sleeping. A host of demons causes landslides, falling rocks, and floods.

All over, both night and day, we find the undead wandering about, crooked surveyors who were murdered and suicides. The Wild Hunt travels widely—it bears a thousand and one names depending on the country or region of Europe in which it appears. Everywhere dwarves and brownies are frolicking, as well as fairies and *jetins, sotrés,* and *courils, lutons* and *ozegans, loutarnes* and *lamigna,* and *fadettes* and *mourmouses.*

France is no different from any other country in this respect. Hungary, for example, has the *tapio,* a sylvan being; the *sarkany,* which corresponds to the drac; the *pörtmandli,* a spirit that haunts mine galleries; and the *szépassny,* beautiful but alas malevolent ladies.[12] During the daytime, the Romanian *zburator* haunts hollow trees.[13] In Walachia, the "wood woman" (*muma padurii*) appears in the dark corners of the forest and "little folk" (*sameni micuti*) come out in the mines. The surrounding world in all German-speaking lands is just as heavily populated. Here we have the *Drach* (drac), the *Schrat* ("howler"), the *Kobold,* the *Hee-mann* (a "calling spirit"), and the *Saligen* (benevolent fairies) alternating with the *Bilwiz* (a kind of dwarf), the famous iron-nosed *Percht,* the *Gonger* (revenants), and the *Huckup,* a spirit that hops on your back and only leaves when you arrive home. Nixies and undines also abound. In Scandinavian countries we find the ladies of the wood (*skogsnuva*), Tom Thumb–like creatures (*pyssling*), the *rå* (numinous powers), the people of the mounds and hills (*haugfolk, tuftefolk*), underground beings (*underjordiske*), the nixies (*näck*), and the undines (*stromkarl, fossegrim*). In the British Isles we have the brownie and the Scottish *ourisk,* Robin Goodfellow, Hudhart, Dobie, and all those who are euphemistically referred to as the Good Neighbors or the Silent Folk.

Lists like this can be drawn up for every country, but to do so is hardly necessary as the point is now quite clear: human beings are not the only intelligent and reasoning beings on earth. Mankind cohabits with other creatures and entities whose presence and existence requires an explanation. It should also be self-evident that all these beings listed above are not recent creations: their names may be but they themselves are ecotypical forms of much older creatures and beliefs.

The extremely important role played by the distribution of space, its division into specific areas, is readily apparent. There is a very clear-cut opposition between civilized space—that of cities, towns, castles, villages, and cultivated lands—and the wild spaces like moors, forests, mountains, marshes, and the sea. These latter places are the natural home and refuge for our unknown or poorly known neighbors. This allocation demands an explanation, as does too the form taken by said neighbors as giants or dwarves, fairies, or marvelous and even terrifying beasts. We will begin, therefore, by examining the myth of the original peopling of the earth.

2

The First Inhabitants of the Earth

If man imagines himself to be an intruder upon the earth, it is because he finds traces of its first inhabitants almost everywhere. Certainly, his conviction is based on what he interprets as remnants, but it primarily derives from experience: the spirits are there; we must come to terms with them. The existence of cultic practices in this regard clearly shows that a confrontation was involved and not merely an act of memory.

This is a fundamental vision of the world that is clearly expressed through the cosmogonies of many peoples, which are then codified in the mythology. There are certainly numerous definitions for the word "mythology," each more scholarly than the last, so it seems helpful in the context of the present study to go back to the original meaning of the word. Mythology is a discourse, therefore the fruit of a way of thinking and of a civilization, and in this sense it gives form to pre-existing, often disparate elements, among which beliefs occupy a central place. Mythology provides evidence of course, but evidence to be handled cautiously, for it is never firsthand and represents one stage in the evolution of beliefs; sometimes it even signals their death. It is nonetheless unavoidable for an investigation of the type I am undertaking here. Mythology also conveys extremely old fossilized notions that it reworks, remodels, or renovates—because the stories it tells deliver some essential truths—which are then inscribed in the order of the world as envisioned by the one god, or the many gods, or by some supernatural agency that gives order to original chaos. Mythology, both Christian and pagan, is therefore a scholarly, artistically sculpted account that is rich in inventions intended to connect the scattered limbs of the beliefs it gathers and to give them consistency, or else restore their coherence. It is therefore necessary to ceaselessly cross-check the information that we glean from mythology with the help of material that comes through other channels.

Many texts state that the first inhabitants of the earth were giants or gigantic humans. According to Hesiod, the Titans, offspring of the union of Heaven and Earth (Ouranos and Gaia), mounted an assault against the heavens but were defeated by the Olympians and then cast down into Tartarus. To avenge them, Gaia gave birth to terrifying, enormous, hairy, bearded giants, but the gods with their ally Hercules defeated them. These giants had serpent legs, but this detail vanished when the two attacks against Olympus became commingled. The memory of this revolt lingered on, so to speak, in all medieval clerical literature and was used to illustrate the sin of pride.[1]

The Bible (Genesis 6:4) claims the giants were born from the intercourse of angels with the descendants of Cain, but commentators and exegetes—along with Saint Augustine—rebuffed this assertion by supporting the opposite claim that giants were around long before angels came to earth. According to a tradition recorded by Walter Map (ca. 1135–1210), archdeacon of Oxford, Adam was of giant-stature, an opinion voiced earlier in the tenth century by Ibrahim ben Wasif Shah in an Arabic treatise titled *The Summary of Wonders*.[2] Medieval encyclopedias also say that the enormous footprint of Adam can be seen in Ceylon at the top of the mountain bearing his name, as this was where he fell upon being expelled from paradise. According to Hebrew traditions, once on earth, Adam's size came down to two hundred and seventy cubits, which is close to five hundred feet! Other Hebrew traditions claim that the men who sought to climb the Tower of Babel to attack God were turned into the demons known as the *Shedim* and the *Lilin*. In the Ethiopian *Book of Enoch,* demons are the spirits of the giants destroyed by God.

In the literature of antiquity and in the Bible, the discovery of the remains of prehistoric animals played a decisive role because these bones were interpreted as being those of giants. Empedocles (ca. 492–432 BCE) speaks of such a discovery. Herodotus of Halicarnassus (ca. 485–430 BCE) tells how the coffin of Orestes, some six cubits long, was exhumed in Tegea in the Peloponnesus (*Histories,* 1, 68). Pausanias describes the discovery of the skeleton of Ajax, the hero of the Trojan War. It measured ten rods; in other words, almost thirty-nine feet. Saint Augustine mentions the discovery of an enormous "human" tooth that had the volume of one hundred ordinary teeth. Around 1250, the Dominican theologian and author Thomas of Cantimpré spoke of the discovery of the bones of Theutanus, the eponymous ancestor of the Teutons, on the banks of the Danube near Vienna (*De natura rerum* III, 5, 40), and Vincent de Beauvais mentions the remains of a giant fifty cubits long (*Speculum naturale,* XXXI, 125). We should note that Theutanus measured ninety-five cubits—in other words, one hundred and fifty-five feet—and his teeth were wider than a palm (almost three inches)! I should add that on January 16, 1613, the bones of King Teutobochus were said to have been unearthed on the so-called Field of Giants (Dauphiné, France). For his part, Bocaccio interpreted the bones found near Palermo and Trapani (Sicily) as those of the Cyclops Polyphemus, but we know today that they belong to a race of dwarf elephants.[3] A mammoth femur hung from the portal of Saint Stephen's Cathedral in Vienna was claimed to be that of a giant.

Throughout nearly the whole of Europe, megalithic monuments were attributed to giants since only a colossal strength could have created them, or so it was believed. In Germany there are the megalithic burial sites known as the "Giants' Tombs" (*Hünengräber*) and even

"Giants' Beds" (*Hünenbedde*) in the region of the Weser. In Denmark, we have the *jaettestuer,* the "Chambers of the Giants." The cromlech of Stonehenge in England was the subject of many medieval legends. According to Geoffrey of Monmouth (ca. 1100–1155) and the Anglo-Norman chronicler Wace (ca. 1110–1174), the enchanter Merlin transported these stones to this location from Ireland. Giants of ancient times had placed them in their baths because of their healing properties. Merlin allegedly found them on Mount Kildare (*Historia regum Britanniae,* VII, 11). Gerald of Wales tells us of a Circle of Giants in the Irish plain of Kildare, not far from Naas (*Topographia Hibernica,* II, 18).

These examples reveal how tangible reality lent strength to our ancestors' belief in giants. The attribution of megalithic monuments to these creatures gave birth to a widespread myth about giant builders, which is often mentioned by the literature of entertainment. The Anglo-Saxon poem *The Ruin* attributes the remnants of ancient civilizations to them:

> *Wondrous is this stone wall, shattered by fate. . . .*
> *The buildings of the city have fallen, the work of giants*
> *   decays.*

In *Aymeri de Narbonne,* an early thirteenth-century *chanson de geste,* giants built the cities of Esclabarie, Montirant, and Cordre. In the twelfth-century romance *Les Quatre Fils Aymon* (The Four Sons of Aymon), it is said that the giant Fortibias fortified the site of Vaucouleurs, and it appears that the previously mentioned castle of Tintagel was the work of his ancestors.[4] La Turbie in Provence is the *tourre dou gigant* (Giant's Tower). For its part, a thirteenth-century Anglo-Norman poem, *Des grants geanz* (Of the Great Giants), states that giants were present on the earth before the birth of Christ.[5] And in Chrétien de Troyes's *Perceval, Le Conte de Graal* (Perceval, the Story of the Grail), we read:

toz li roiaumes de Logres
*qui jadis fu la terre as ogres . . .**

According to the *Prose Edda* written by the great Icelandic poet and mythographer Snorri Sturluson (1178/9–1241), the gods of the Norse pantheon entrusted a giant with the task of fortifying their domain of Asgard, but the builder demanded in payment the Sun, the Moon, and Freyja, and the gods were only able to get out of this fix thanks to the cunning Loki (*Gylfaginning,* chap. 42).

Germanic traditions are marked by the same idea of primordial giants, but have the merit of being more explicit. According to Snorri Sturluson, in the chaos of the beginning there was an unfathomable abyss filled with the ice of the North and the fire of the Sun. The heat caused the ice to melt and a giant named Ymir emerged. From him was spawned the race of giants called the Rime Thurses. He was provided food by the cow Audumla, who was born in the same way. By licking the frost-covered stones, she caused the emergence of a man, Buri, who then himself engendered—because all these primordial beings are hermaphrodites—a son named Borr who married a giant's daughter named Bestla, and they had three sons: Odin, the supreme god of the Germanic pantheon, Vili, and Vé. In this tradition, giants are not only the first inhabitants of the world; they are also the fathers of the gods. Furthermore, the earth was created from Ymir's body: his body was the land; his blood was the sea and lakes; his bones, the mountains; his teeth, the mounds of pebbles and stones; and his skull, the celestial vault. The gods only created humans sometime later, but the giants did not disappear.

This view of things is shared by Saxo Grammaticus in his *Gesta danorum* (History of the Danes), written around 1200, but its mythological information is rationalized in the style of Euhemerus. Three races stronger than men appeared in succession: first were the giants, then the sorcerers (meaning the gods), who were weaker physically but supe-

---

*All the kingdom of Logres / was once the land of ogres . . .

rior in intelligence and magical technique. They defeated the giants and passed themselves off as gods. There was finally the race born from the crossbreeding of the first two, which were deified by ignorant humans. Saxo never says where humans sprang from, since as a good Christian he could not cite Eddic traditions and hoped that Adam—the "father of us all," as was said in those times—would come to the mind for his readers. The *Heldenbuch* (Book of Heroes), printed in Strassburg around 1483, states in its prose preface that the earth was first inhabited by dwarves and then giants, whose mission was to protect them from the huge dragons.[6]

The scholars of ancient times vacillated between dwarves and giants as our planet's primordial inhabitants, but this hesitation quickly ended when the Bible became the ultimate authority in all Christendom. In the prologue to his *History of the Danes,* Saxo Grammaticus provides a good example of a blend of real, mythical, and Christian elements:

> That the Danish area was once cultivated by a civilisation of giants is testified by the immense stones attached to ancient barrows and caves. If anyone is doubtful whether or not this was executed by superhuman force, let him gaze at the height of certain mounds and then say, if he can, who carried such enormous boulders to their summits. . . . There is too little evidence to decide whether those who contrived these works were giants who lived after the irruption of the Flood or men of preternatural strength. Such creatures, so our countrymen maintain, are today supposed to inhabit the rugged, inaccessible waste-land which I have mentiond above and be endowed with transmutable bodies, so that they have the incredible power of appearing and disappearing, of being present and suddenly somewhere else.[7]

This short passage provides some valuable information. First is the fact that giants survived the great flood, an opinion shared by Werner of Basel in the eleventh century (*Synodicus,* v. 104–9);[8] next is the fact that the megalithic monuments are the work of giants. Finally it shows that these individuals are more than oversized humans and possess supernatural powers like being able to move instantaneously over great distances and to become invisible at will. This confirms that Saxo was speaking of a supernatural race called "Giants" and not giants as we customarily imagine them.

The Celts, whose ancient Irish literature offers our best evidence, conceived the peopling of green Erin as a succession of invasions.[9] The first race settled there before the Deluge and vanished with it. A race led by Parthalon arrived next and cleared the land, but they had to contend with the Fomorians, brutal and greedy giants who dwelt in these isles before they were cruelly wiped out by a sudden pestilence. They were followed by the race of Nemed who paid heavy tribute to the Fomorians before vanishing in turn. Next came the Fir Bolg, who perished when the Tuatha Dé Danann, the owners of marvelous talismans and the keepers of magical secrets, invaded the island. The Tuatha Dé Danann also encountered the Fomorians and were compelled to accept the rule of kings born from their intermarriages with this race before they were evicted by the sons of Mil, the ancestors of the Gaelic people. The Tuatha Dé Danann then moved underground into the caves and mounds where they still live. They are invisible when they travel through their former domains, still retain great power, and can do great favors for people as well as great harm.[10] It is easy to see the implication of these facts: the underground world is inhabited by the gods or their descendants,* and their world opens at regular intervals such as Samain (November 1), for example. Furthermore, anyone who ventures into a cave or any other excavation into the earth can very easily find himself in their realm.[11]

---

*According to the *Serglige Con Culainn* (The Wasting Sickness of Cú Chulainn), "the diabolical power was great before the faith [Christianity], it was so great that devils used to fight with men in bodily form, and used to show delights and mysteries to them, as though they really existed. So they were believed to be; and ignorant men used to call those visions *síde* and *áes síde*" (§49; trans. Myles Dillon). The *síde* are the mounds, the underground kingdoms; later, through metonymy, the term came to refer to the Celtic fairies.

It should not be assumed that these opinions about the original populating of the earth are exclusive to the Medieval West—similar concepts can be found in Arabic literature of the Middle Ages. In the thirteenth century, the great encyclopaedist Zakariya al-Qazwini (died 1283) concentrated his study on living creatures and provided us with these interesting bits of information:

> There is a common legend that maintains that the race of *djinn* were, long before the creation of Adam, the inhabitants of the earth. These beings covered the dry land, the sea, the plains and the mountains. . . . They had a government, prophets, a religion and laws, but they were swallowed by their pride and rebelled; they stopped heeding the laws of their prophets and caused many misfortunes upon the land. The God, the All-Powerful, sent down a troop of angels to dwell upon the earth where they chased them to the shores of islands and captured a great many of them.[12]

Ibrahim ben Wasif Shah's *Summary of Wonders* tells this same story but with less detail: God created the earth and then He placed upon it races of genies who extolled His glory and holiness constantly; once they ceased to do this, He punished them. Behind all these legends we find the same element that can also be seen in Greco-Roman mythology: the original inhabitants of the earth rebelled against God or the gods.

With this observation we are entering into the sphere of religious interpretation. At one time firmly rooted in spirits, the belief in great ancestors—which may involve the remnants of a race of giants or of gods; the former being great in size, the latter possessed of great intelligence and magic—is recuperated by the prevailing religion, which provides an explanation of this belief in a way that has twofold importance. First, these beings are demonized and likened to monsters because deformity is an undeniable mark of sin by virtue of a postulate that maintains physical appearance is a reflection of the soul. These beings were then banished to specific places—but precisely those locations to which medieval beliefs and legends clung. A treatise on the origins of the human race inserted into the *Lebor na hUidre* (Book of the Dun Cow), written in Ireland around 1100, includes a chapter entitled "The History of Monsters: The Fomorians and the Dwarves," which tells what led Noah to curse his son Ham and goes on to say:

> Ham was the first man to be struck by a curse since the Flood. From him are born the dwarves, the fomorians, the goat-headed men, and all deformed beings that exist among men.[13]

A clarification should be made here. In the Middle Ages, the term "giant" functioned as a cover term that applied to various creatures, individuals of large size, spirits, and genies. In fact, "giant" designates a primordial race whose size is not necessarily immense, and which consisted of several "clans." In Scandinavia there were thus the *þursar,* the *jötnar,* and the *risar,* whose traces can also be found in Britain and Germany, and their perpetual war against the gods can be seen as a war waged for possession of a territory by two different ethnic groups. Furthermore, there are small "giants"—Reginn in the legend of Sigurðr/Siegfried, for example. Moreover, large dwarves such as Beli and Brians can also be found in Chrétien de Troyes's *Erec et Enide.* Beli and Brians are two brothers; one is the smallest of all dwarves, the other is a palm larger than all the largest men. The traces of these combinations of dwarves, giants, and land spirits, and the uncertainty surrounding the morphology of these individuals, are clearly confirmed in the most recent folklore.

Medieval literature was greatly influenced by that of classical antiquity, and by the writings of the early Church Fathers, and the revolt of the "giants" is constantly referred to as an illustration of the sin of pride. It is therefore probable that the authority of these writings played a prominent role in the reduction of the number and the names of the world's first inhabitants, and in the projection of the autochthonous elements onto the figure of the giant.

3

Demons
and Fallen Angels

While numerous narratives, including many collected recently by folk-lorists, describe giants as the first inhabitants of the earth, there are other texts that indicate they were preceded by angels. The universe is therefore populated by beings that are not members of the human race. They are known under different names—dragons, gods, spirits, demons, or fallen angels—that designate them collectively. It is therefore necessary to see where they dwell and conceal themselves. The majority of texts are quite clear on this point and this unanimity is quite revealing: similar thought patterns are encountered, regardless of any differences in ethnicity or civilization.

According to Hebrew traditions, demons preferred to haunt isolated, remote, or unclean places: ruins, the desert, latrines.[1] They are far from harmless and will attack both man and beast. They cause both physical and mental illnesses and are especially dreadful at night. In Islamic traditions, the *shayātīn* (satans) and *djinn* hide in caves, swamps, mountains, valleys, thickets, and deserts.[2] In fact, they had been banished by God, and the angels who carried out His sentence drove them into the "confines of the isles." Iblis, the prince of the *djinn,* asked God for a meeting place and He gave them the crossroads and marketplaces.

In the deserts we find the *ghūl,* in the thickets we find the *si'la;* the *udar* are on the coasts of Yemen and the *dalhāt* on the isles of the sea. This is why it is not surprising to read in travelers' tales how—driven off course by a storm—men were cast up on unknown shores where they had great difficulty escaping the *djinn.* The isles of the Green Sea—meaning the outer sea—and the Sea of Darkness—meaning the ocean—as well as the Wāq-Wāq, a fabled land that was sometimes the mainland and sometimes an island located at the edge of the world, served as the ulti-mate lair of these malefic creatures. In these two civilizations (Hebrew and Islamic), demons live on the margins of the civilized space, and Yahuz (died 808) even said that *djinn* occupied the land of the Wabar when God sought to slay them and defended it against those lusting for it. This was again reiterated by Yaqut al-Hamawi (1179–1229) who adds the detail that this land extends between the dunes of Yabrîn and Yemen, and that "no one lives there."

Out of necessity or, if you prefer, by divine decree the *djinn* thus became the genies of specific places, as this example clearly shows. The historian and poet Abu Al-Faraj Al-Isfahani (897–967) tells how they killed two people who had burned the trees of a piece of land and cul-tivated it. (The reader should keep this bit of information in mind for later.) Ibn Hisham (died 828 or 833) recorded the phrase used by trav-eling Arabs when planning to camp for the night in a valley: "I place myself under the protection of the *djinni,* the master of this valley, so that he will protect me from any evil that may befall during this night!" There is therefore means of neutralizing the *djinn,* or at least appealing to their good natures, which shows that not all of them are demons. Ali ibn al-Athir (1160–ca. 1233) and Zakariya al-Qazwini tell how a wolf made off with a lamb from the flock of a shepherd who shouted: "O demon of the vale! He heard a voice cry out: 'Wolf, return his lamb to him!' And the wolf returned it and went away." Narratives like this show that a religious interpretation has been superimposed over a much older belief that the land belongs to genies who also have command over animals.

The medieval West fashioned its own vision of things. Fed on biblical traditions and elements of local paganism, the Church created a myth, that of the neutral angels, which takes place in the circle of influence of the story told in Genesis. Taking their cue from Saint Justin (ca. 114–165), some Greek apologists repeated the fable that claimed giants (*Nephilim*) or demons were born from the congress of fallen angels and the daughters of men. Their spirits lurked among men seeking to send them astray from God. They are the source of magic, idolatry, and all the vices. Saint Irenaeus (ca. 130–202) and Tertullian (ca. 155–220) were inspired by this tradition, and Lactantius (ca. 260–325) tells us that from the fallen angels were born the "celestial demons" and from them the "earthly demons," and they are the unclean spirits who wander the earth.[3] Saint Augustine (354–430) provides one final important detail: "the gods of the nations are most impure demons, who desire to be thought gods, availing themselves of the names of certain defunct souls, or the appearance of mundane creatures."[4] The testimonies cited above provide the backbone for the medieval explanation of demons.

But what is to be said about all these little spirits of the land that in antiquity were labeled fauns, sylvan creatures, satyrs, and so forth, and which in the Middle Ages were called sprites, dwarves, incubi, and succubi? The interpretations of Lactantius and Saint Augustine combine to form a belief attested to by Martianus Capella in the fifth century:

> The places inaccessible to men are inhabited by a host of *very ancient* creatures [my italics] who haunt woods, glades, and groves, and lakes and springs, and brooks; whose names are Pans, Fauns, *Fontes,* Satyrs, Sylvans, Nymphs, *Fatui* or *Fantuae,* or even *Fanae.*[5]

In the sixth century, bishop Martin of Braga (Portugal) spoke of the angels who fell from heaven with Lucifer. He stated:

> Many are those who remain in the sea, the rivers, the springs, or the forests; ignorant folk worship them as gods and offer them sacrifices.

In the sea they invoke Neptune; in the rivers, the Lamias; in the springs, the nymphs; and in the forests, the Dianas, who are naught but demons and evil spirits who oppress the faithless men who know not enough to defend themselves with the sign of the cross.[6]

In the twelfth century, Hugh of Pisa wrote this in his etymological work *Magnae derivationes:*

Many of the demons expelled from heaven live in the sea, the rivers, the springs, or the forests; the ignorant call them almost gods and offer them sacrifices. In the sea they are called Neptune, Lamia in the rivers, Nymphs in the fountains, and Diana in the forests.[7]

Things took clearer shape between the sixth and twelfth centuries and a more canonical explanation was offered. One group of angels took no part in the struggle that pitted God against Lucifer. As their sin was lesser than that of the rebel angels, God cast them down on earth and not into hell. This legend is outlined in the Irish story of the *Voyage of Saint Brendan,* and it appears in Germanic regions in Wolfram von Eschenbach's *Parzival,* in the French *Chanson d'Esclarmonde,* and in the *South English Legendary* (ca. 1280–1290). We even find it in the *Register* of the Inquisitor Jacques Fournier, who was charged with wiping out the Cathar heresy during the fourteenth century.[8]

So what became of these angels who were cast down to earth? They became the spirits who hid in wild, virgin nature.* Let's look at the account of one of them, collected by Gerald of Wales in his *Journey Through Wales* at the end of the twelfth century:

A stranger attached himself to the bishop of Dacia and told him one day: "Before Jesus Christ was born in the flesh," he said, "but when

---

*Comparison with other pagan traditions allows a glimpse of a mythic archetype. In Lithuania, for example, Giraitis watches over the woods, Upinis over the rivers, Ezerinis over the lakes, and the Laukasargai watch over the fields.

He came, this power was greatly diminished. They were dispersed, some here, some there, for they fled headlong from his presence. Some hurled themselves into the sea. Others hid in hollow trees and in the cracks of rocks. I remember that I myself jumped down a well."[9]

Walter Map displays his erudition when recording the following in his *De nugis curialium* (Trifles of Courtiers). The rebel angels were cast down on earth, "sometimes in vast deserts, and sometimes in inhabited places, depending on their sin." Deceived by the devil, our ancestors believed these were demigods and demigoddesses (*semideos aut semideas*) and, based on where they lived, "they were called Hill-creatures, Sylvans, Dryads, Oreads, Fauns, Satyrs, and Naiads" (IV, 6). The beginning of this list was probably borrowed from Ovid (*Metamorphoses,* I, 190ff) but the terms used here mask local realities, at least partially. Gervase of Tilbury says of the spirits called sprites: "They slip into stones and woods" (*Otia Imperialia,* I, 18).

A thirteenth-century German text titled *Magnificat* has the value of using the folk names of demons based on their habitat:

God cast the demons to earth. They are everywhere. In the waters and the mountains dwell the *Nicker* and the dwarves, in the forests and marshes God has also placed the little Hairy Ones (?); these are the elves, the *Thurses* and the *Wichte,* who are worth nothing at all.[10]

The *Nicker* are nixies or sirens, the *Thurses* are giants, and *Wichte* (wights) is a generic term for those whose name one does not wish or dare to speak out loud. We can therefore see that corresponding to the Latin terms *Lamia, Neptunus, gigas, spiritus,* and so on are spirits of the folk traditions, the beings of popular mythology.

It is extremely important to avoid clinging to the clerical interpretation that characterizes the whole of the European Middle Ages. For more than fifteen years I have been lifting a corner of the veil through a series of studies that have allowed me to show on numerous occasions that the Latin names—which represent a tributary of the traditions of classical antiquity and the *interpraetatio christiana*—are deceptive because they are approximations of the indigenous spirits' names. This point is extremely important and has stirred up many difficulties for those seeking to grasp what the Latin terms are concealing. It is enough to recall the passage by Saxo Grammaticus given earlier in which the term "giants" (*gigantes*) clearly overlies that of the Thurses, mythological figures as depicted in the *Eddas,* or perhaps Trolls, which the Church transformed into demons, as shown by this saying, *"Troll hafi þik!"* meaning "May the Devil carry you off!"

The majority of demons therefore dwell in remote, desolate areas, and the legend of the origin of the Huns is built on this motif. According to Jordanes, the historian of the Goths, King Filimer expelled witches called *Haliurunnae* into the deserts. They mated with the demons living there and gave birth to the Huns. This legend was very popular and can be found scattered throughout the scholarly and historical literature. In France, for example, Lambert of Saint-Omer echoed it in his *Liber floridus* (Book of Flowers).

4

Cult Remnants

The writs of the councils and synods, the lives of the saints, and the homilies and sermons of the early Middle Ages are all in agreement on one point: the conversion of pagans to Christianity was quite flawed and did not serve to eradicate various diabolical, sacrilegious, and highly condemnable practices.[1] It so happens that among these practices the worship given to certain places, or which occured in certain places, played a significant role. The fact that these locations were always the same is something that requires our attention.

Around 563, Gregory of Tours condemned the laxity of priests who tolerated the persistence of a worship of stones, trees, and springs, "places designated by the pagans." The *Epistola canonica,* which dates from the sixth century, speaks of "these unreasonable men who worship springs and trees," which the Council of Agde banned in 506, whereas the penitentials called for a penance of three years on bread and water for those who worship at such places. Caesarius of Arles (470–542) was hindered by his flock who refused to abandon ancestral practices and would not chop down and burn the sacred trees, or cease speaking vows at the springs and fountains, or frequenting sanctuaries that would be rebuilt as fast as they were torn down. "None should worship trees" is an order that Caesarius repeated tirelessly. "If you still see people worshipping trees or springs," he said elsewhere, "condemn them

harshly, for whoever commits this sin loses the sacrament of baptism."
Indefatigable, he returned to the charge: "I again urge you to destroy
all pagan sanctuaries wherever you find them; do not pray by wells and
springs. . . . If someone knows that pagan altars or sanctuaries are near
his home, or trees that receive pagan worship, may he strive to knock
them down or into many pieces, or cut them off at the root."[2] It would
not be hard to provide another thousand examples that say the same
thing from other authors throughout the medieval West.

In 658 the Synod of Nantes spoke of sacred trees and indicated
that no one dared cut a branch or even a shoot, and the people,
deceived by the devil, "worshipped the stones in ruinous places and
in the forests." A Carolingian sermon mentions "the sacred trees of
Jupiter and Mercury," a description that of course conceals other deities with only an extremely remote connection with the Roman gods
whose names are being used here. However, Roman and Christian
interpretation was omnipresent and covered up the indigenous traditions. The eighth-century *Homilia de sacrilegiis* (Homily on the
Sacrileges) informs us that Christians observed the Neptunalia (July
23) near fountains, rivers, and the sea. The list of sites is completed
by the *Vita S. Eligii* (Life of Saint Eligius), written in the seventh century by Audoin, who added the boundaries, borders, and crossroads
where candles are lit and offerings made, something already indicated
by Pirmin of Reichenau in an eloquent passage:

> Do not worship idols, stones, trees, remote places, wells, or the inter-
> sections of roads. Do not put yourself in the hands of enchanters,
> sorcerers, magicians, haruspices, seers, magicians, and spellcasters.
> Do not believe in the magical significance of sneezes, nor the super-
> stitions connected with small birds, nor diabolical charms. Other
> than diabolical worship, what could such things mean as celebrating
> the Vulcanalia, the calends, plaiting laurel wreaths, paying attention
> to the position of the feet, splaying your hand on tree trunks, cast-
> ing bread and wine into springs. . . . Do not hang at crossroads or in

trees wooden replicas of human limbs. . . . No Christian shall sing songs in church, at home, or at the intersections of roads.[3]

The Synod of Szabolcs (Hungary) in 1092 noted the existence of sacrifices to wells, and the treatise *Ratio de cathecizandis rudibus* (Reason to Catechize the Peasantry; written ca. 800 about the means of teaching the gospel to pagans) refers twice to sacrifices made in remote places (*ad angulos*). We also know that these ceremonies were accompanied by sacrificial meals. The *Homily on the Sacrileges* mentions the sacrifice of animals whose flesh was then eaten. These took place "on ancient altars and in sacred groves." Charlemagne's *Capitulatio de Partibus Saxoniae* (Capitulary for the Saxon Regions) from around 785 banned these banquets given "in the honor of demons."

We should take special care to avoid thinking that it was the object—the spring, tree, stone, and so forth—that was worshipped. This is a much too common error. No, it was the power dwelling within the object—the numen, spirit, demon—that was addressed. The Council of Agde expressly states that men believed a numinous being was residing in such places.

We should also avoid becoming bogged down in another error that is regularly repeated. Many scholars believe that the testimony of the ecclesiastical literature is not valid because it attributes a Roman paganism to the peoples of the medieval West and, moreover, that the content of the sermons and penitentials, the acts of councils and synods, in no way reflects reality because they are the product of a self-contained tradition that repeats the same things over and over. Each text is merely a copy of an earlier one and serves as the source from which the clerics in other lands draw their knowledge.

This is partially true, but if we compare these traditions with the accounts from the vernacular literature—which many historians often forget to do, rejecting such texts on the pretext that they are only unrealistic fantasies—we shall find that the catechetical texts are, like the narrative literature, a mirror, albeit a more or less distorted one, of reality. No cleric or writer ventured too far astray from reality; it fed their writings, for just as is the case today, no one invents what one does not know. Analyzing a passage from Pirmin of Reichenau's *Liber scarapsus,* which I cited earlier, Philippe Walter has quite rightly drawn attention to this point:

> Contemporary reality is expressed here under the veil of an ancient culture that contributes to the blurring of certain specific features in order to dissolve them into an obsessional fantasy of universal paganism. It is, however, self-evident that certain practices condemned here must also have been actually observed by the abbot. When reading such a text we must therefore keep in mind that a screen of humanist culture and a topical condemnation was inevitably interposed between what is possible to see and the observer, whose concern was in no way parallel to the relative objectivity of the modern ethnologist.[4]

The lives of the saints exalting Christianity's victories over paganism (among other things) provide complementary information.[5] The sacred trees fell to the axes of the men of God. Sulpicius Severus, bishop of Bourges (584–591), writes about how Saint Martin had a pine or pear tree near a sanctuary chopped down, "because it was dedicated to the devil." Saint Barbatus (died 682), who lived in Benevento under the rule of the kings Grimoald and Romuald, toppled the sacred tree where the Lombards hung the hides of slain animals, meat, and so forth. Saint Amateur (died 418), bishop of Auxerre, uprooted a pine tree on the branches of which the future Saint Germain had hung the heads of the wild animals he had killed hunting. In 725 Saint Boniface chopped down the sacred oak the Hessians worshipped in Geismar and in 772 Charlemagne destroyed the Saxon's Irminsul. In Adam of Bremen's *Gesta ecclesiae Hammaburgensis pontificum* (History of the Archbishops of Hamburg-Bremen), written around 1070, he provides a report about the pagan sanctuary of Uppsala:

Near this temple stands a very large tree with wide-spreading branches, always green both winter and summer. What kind it is nobody knows. There is also a spring at which the pagans are accustomed to make their sacrifices, and into it they plunge a live man. And if he is not found, the people's wish will be granted.[6]

The waters also had their devotees. In the sixth century, Gregory of Tours described the worship dedicated to Lake Saint-Andéol in the Massif Central region of France:

At a fixed time a crowd of rustics went there and, as if offering libations to the lake, threw [into it] linen cloths and garments that served men as clothing. Some [threw] pelts of wool, many [threw] models of cheese and wax and bread as well as various [other] objects, each according to his own means, that I think would take too long to enumerate. They came with their wagons, they brought food and drink, sacrificed animals, and feasted for three days. But before they were due to leave on the fourth day, a violent storm approached them with thunder and lightning. The heavy rainfall and hailstones fell with such force that each person thought he would not escape. Every year this happened this way, but these foolish people were bound up in their mistake.[7]

Such examples are legion and can even be found into more recent times—coins were still tossed into Lake Saint-Andéol in the nineteenth century—even when heavily Christianized. So what were the pagans trying to accomplish through their sacrifices and prayers? At Lake Saint-Andéol, it was rain; elsewhere it was healing, as clearly stated by a Carolingian capitulary. Even if the texts generally remain quite discreet, it is relatively easy to see that the primary considerations were food and health. The hope was to have enough—enough water for the crops and enough sun for them to grow. They also wanted wild game to be plentiful. Neutrality or kindness was desired from the local spirits. People wanted the spirits to leave them alone, which is to say they did not want the spirits to send any illness with their invisible arrows, nor to pester the livestock.

Let us take a look at the Icelandic *Landnámabók* (Book of Settlements)—one version of which, the *Sturlubók,* was written by Sturla Thórðarson (1214–1284)—as it offers us a view of a still living paganism and its information matches that found in the clerical literature.[8] Here is Thórir Snepill of Lundr: "He worshipped a grove of trees" (S 237).* Here is Eyvind, the settler of Flateyardal: "He paid worship to the Stones-of-Gunnr" (S 241). Thorstein Red-Nose worshipped the waterfall near his home; on the night he died, all his sheep fell into the waterfall (S 255). There is a monster in one version of the *Saint Óláf's Saga* that is half-woman and half-whale; "The natives offer her sacrifices and regard her as a good protector of the land."[9]

The Christian laws (*Kristenret*) of the Gulaþing assembly in Norway condemn the pagans for "believing in the land spirits (*landvættir*) whether found in groves or mounds or waterfalls." This is an extremely important observation because it tells us that worship was not addressed to the high gods of the Germanic pantheon, but to the numinous forces closer to man, which therefore held a greater significance for his daily life. The *Gutalagen,* the early lawcode of Gotland, scolds those who say prayers at the groves, *tumuli,* idols, and places surrounded by a fence (*loca palis circumsepta*). It also provides us with two interesting expressions: *trúa á hult* ("to believe in the hills") and *trúa á hauga* ("to believe in the mounds").

This also brings to mind what Tacitus said in his *Germania* about the ancient Germanic tribes: "They consecrate woods and groves, and the mystery that they see only in their awe they call by the names of the gods." And: "From their sacred groves they remove certain images and symbols that they carry into battle."[10]

In the *Pharsalia,* Lucan describes a sacred grove near Marseille that Cæsar had destroyed as follows:

---

* ...ising the following abbreviations for the two texts: H = *Hauksbók;* S = *Sturlubók.*

A grove there was, untouched by men's hands from ancient times, whose interlacing boughs enclosed a space of darkness and cold shade, and banished the sunlight from above. . . . On those boughs— if antiquity, reverential of the gods, deserves any credit—birds feared to perch; in these coverts wild beasts would not lie down; no wind ever bore down upon that wood, nor thunderbolt hurled from the black clouds; the trees, even when they spread their leaves to no breeze, rustled of themselves. Water, also, fell there in abundance from dark springs. The images of the gods, grim and rude, were uncouth blocks formed of felled tree trunks.[11]

Adam of Bremen provides a similar description (I, 7) and he adds: "they even regarded with reverence leafy trees and springs." The pagans, he says a little further on, "they prohibit only, to this very day indeed, access to their groves and springs which, they aver, are polluted by the entry of Christians" (IV, 18).[12] Around 1220, Oliver of Paderborn noted that the Pruthenes (ancient Prussians) worshipped the nymphs of forests and rivers, and, in the middle of the fifteenth century, Jerome of Prague stated they "worshipped trees sacred to demons," especially oaks of great age. The *Hervarar saga ok Heiðreks* (Saga of Hervör and Heidrek) mentions the existence of a tree of sacrifices. Alcuin's *Vita Sancti Willibrordi* (Life of Saint Willibrord) indicates that on the island where the Frisians worshipped the god Fo(r) site, "none of the natives would venture to meddle with any of the cattle that fed there nor with anything else, nor dare they draw water from the spring that bubbled up there except in complete silence."[13] Among the Celts, the Ross Yew, the Mughna Oak, and the Uisnedr Ash attest to similar beliefs,[14] and in France, until quite recently, processions were still made to the oak of Saint Quirin. We should also recall that Joan of Arc was accused of frequenting an old oak beneath whose branches was a fountain, and which was called the Oak of Destiny, or even the Oak of the Bourlemont Fairies.[15]

5

The Local Land Spirits

We shall continue our exploration in the Scandinavian north. Several texts confirm the beliefs we have already encountered in the Mediterranean basin, Great Britain, and Germany. These texts are important because they cannot be relegated to the list of wonders and fantasies that were so abundant in the Middle Ages. One of the oldest accounts, that of Ari the Wise (Ari Thorgilsson; 1067–1148) to whom we owe the *Íslendingabók,* cites the Laws of Úlfljót, which stated:

> No ships adorned with wooden images of heads should be used on the open seas; however, if this rule was not followed, the image was at least to be removed before the ship made landfall so that it would not sail up to the shore with gaping head and beak and thus frighten the guardian spirits of the country.[1]

The *Book of Settlements* says the same thing (H 268) and other texts—such as the *Þórðar saga hreðu* (Saga of Thord the Red) and *Þorsteins þáttr Uxafóts* (Tale of Thorstein Oxfoot)—corroborate this clear and specific testimony: every country has its spirits. When Egil Skallagrímsson attacks King Eirik Bloodaxe, he performs a magical operation intended to remove the protection of the local spirits from his victim:

36

Egil went ashore onto the island, picked up a branch of hazel and went to a certain cliff that faced the mainland. Then he took a horse head, set it up on the pole and spoke these formal words (*formáli*): "Here I set a pole of insult (*níðstöng*) against King Eirik and Queen Gunnhild"—then, turning the horse head towards the mainland— "and I direct this insult against the guardian spirits (*landvættir*) of this land, so that every one of them shall go astray, neither to figure nor find their dwelling places until they have driven King Eirik and Queen Gunnhild from this country.

Next he jammed the pole into a cleft in the rock and left it standing there with the horse head facing towards the mainland, and cut runes on the pole declaiming the words of his formal speech (*formáli*).[2]

The spell was successful and King Eirik and his wife were soon forced to leave the country.

When King Harald Gormsson of Denmark decided to take possession of Iceland, he consulted a magician who possessed the power to send a double (alter ego) of himself great distances so he could obtain information about conditions on the island. Snorri Sturluson, who tells this story in the *Saint Óláf's Saga,* writes:

He went in a whale's-shape. And when he came to Iceland he proceeded west and north around it. He saw that all the mountains and hills were full of land-wights (*landvættir*), some big and some small. And when he came to the Vápnafjord he swam into the fjord, intending to go ashore there. Then a big dragon came down the valley, followed by many serpents, toads, and adders that blew poison against him. Then he swam away, heading west along the land, all the way to the Eyjafjord, and then he entered into that fjord. Then there flew against him a bird so large that its wings touched the mountains on either side of the fjord, and a multitude of other birds besides, both large and small. Away he backed from there, swimming west around the land and then south to Breithafjord and entered that fjord. There came against him a big bull, wading out into the water and bellowing fearfully. A multitude of land-wights (*landvættir*) followed him. Away he backed from there, swimming around Reykjaness, and intended to come ashore at Víkarssekeith. Then came against him a mountain giant with an iron bar in his hand, and his head was higher than the mountains, and many other giants were with him.[3]

For those familiar with Norse traditions, it is obvious that the island is inhabited by local land spirits (*landvættir*) who can assume animal shape, a detail given copious illustration here and of major importance for comprehension of more recent folk beliefs and traditions in which quite often the local spirit is zoomorphic. This is the case, for example, with the Icelandic *Vatnahestur,* the Water Horse, a spirit that tends to lakes. But this vision of things can also be found elsewhere, and the Scottish *kelpie* is an exact equivalent of the *Vatnahestur.*

The multiplicity of forms assumed by land spirits clearly shows that they are primarily natural forces, *numens* that can incarnate in any creature or even any object they choose, either dwelling within it or possessing it. When this force wishes to show itself to human beings, it seems that it may be obliged to assume the appearance of a locally known creature, but its behavior or color clearly indicate that it is a supernatural being. Moreover, it suggests the paganism of ancient times: in the *Þiðranda þáttr ok Þórhalls* (Story of Thidrand and Thorhall), shortly before Iceland adopted Christianity, the seer Thorhall has a vision: "he sees how many graves have opened and leaving from them is all that lived there, large and small." The underlying meaning is that these are land spirits (*landvættir*).[4]

Let's take another example that shows the many forms land spirits can assume. In his *History of the Danes,* Saxo Grammaticus recounts the voyage of Thorkillus to the Other World, represented here by the territory of the giants Guthmundus and Geruthus. During the time he sailed, the foodstuffs ran out, but a land soon came into view that was rich in cattle. Thorkillus warned his companions, when they came onshore, that they should not slaughter more of the animals than necessary, so as to avoid irritating the guardian deities of the place (*dei loci praeses*) who would not then allow them to leave. His advice went unheeded, "spirits" appeared in various forms and held back the ships, and the travelers were forced to sacrifice one man per ship in order to again set sail.[5]

Wild man and woman. Illustration from The Travels of Sir John Mandeville. *Basel: Bernhard Richel, 1480–1481.*

6

The Underside of Idolatry

It is quite difficult to know today how various idols—whether German, Roman, or Celtic—discussed in the texts were represented, even if they were to be found everywhere. And there are some we need not consider, such as the Saxon Irminsul, which is a depiction of the cosmic tree (Yggdrasill in Scandinavian mythology) and thereore does not fall under the category of an idol since it primarily represents an *axis mundi.* The same probably holds true for many sacred trees, despite the fact that missionaries may have claimed such trees were sacred to a "great god." The testimonies on this point are scarcely reliable and the fact that the "great god" in question is never named suggests that actually some other idol was being worshipped. It is also fairly difficult to know if the idols represented gods or land spirits. What do the twelve satellite stones of the Irish idol, Cromm Cruaich, which form a cromlech on the field of Mag Slecht, actually mean? The central idol Cromm Cruaich "gave peace and power to each of the provinces. . . . The brave Goidels worshipped it and asked it for good weather. . . . For it, without glory, they slew their first-born children. . . . They asked of it milk and wheat in return for their infants."[1]

It is certainly possible that land spirits and gods were associated

40

with one another, at least this is what is suggested by the text preserved for us on an *ex-voto*. An inscription found in Mainz and dated 211 AD is addressed to the "Aufaniae goddesses and the protectors of the site" (*et tutelae loci;* CIL 13: 6665).[2] Another inscription, dating from the second century, is dedicated "to great Jupiter and the spirit of the place (*et genio loci;* CIL 13: 7789). Siegfried Gutenbrunner's precise, meticulous study of the inscriptions found in the German regions has shown that many gods or goddesses were inextricably connected with a specific place, and thus were originally land spirits.[3] The goddesses Ahueccaniae, Aveha, and Helliseva were probably those of springs; the matrons Textumeihae and Mediotoutehae were the guardians of Pagus Textumis and Pagus Mediotoutus; the name Nemetocenna, associated with a city in Belgian Gaul, is derived from *nemeton,* meaning "sacred grove."

There is another track that suggests a hodgepodge made up of gods and local spirits. The vocabulary used by the cleric Reginon of Prüm (died 915) says that the trees are sacred "to demons," *daemonibus,* a plural dative case, which refers to an undifferentiated entity. The *Homily on the Sacrileges* mentions people who bring any kind of iron object into their house "because they fear demons," again a plural generic term. The Styrian penitential that Burchard of Worms repeated in his *Decretum* (ca. 1010) mentions the people who dare not leave home before cockcrow, "because the vile spirits then have greater power to harm than afterward." It is clear that "demon" and "vile spirit" would not designate gods. These are blanket terms that are being used to refer to wights and demonized spirits. They happen to be connected to places—trees, houses, and so on—and, since the night belongs to them, it gives them the liberty to go where they wish, whereas during the day they remain stuck in place.

In reality, this restriction comes from the fact that they are the opposite of God and light, and therefore belong to the devil and darkness. This is a claim that needs to be viewed cautiously, however, since there are legitimate grounds for wondering if the opposition of clarity and darkness is not due to Christianity. (An exception would be the case of dwarves who are sometimes petrified when caught in the light of day; this belief does not seem to be the result of any Christian influence.) Martin of Braga expressly says that the Neptunes of the sea, the Lamia of the rivers, the Nymphs of the fountains, and the Dianas of the forest are all "demons and evil spirits" (*maligni daemones et spiritus*). Burchard of Worms supplies one additional detail: these spirits that haunt houses, and to whom he gives the Roman names of satyrs and hairy ones, were the recipients of offerings intended to earn prosperity and wealth from them.[4]

It is questionable whether we should take literally commands by clerics such as "You should not worship idols," for that is a way of saying "do not be idolatrous," meaning "do not practice any pagan worship." A passage by Pirmin of Reichenau speaks in favor of this interpretation: "You must not worship *the idols*"—I underscore this term, which means, in fact, "false gods"—"nor on the stones, the trees, the nooks, and the wells." Compare this tirade to that of a penitential: "If you come upon these places . . . namely, fountains, stones, trees, or crossroads." What emerges from all this is the fact we must avoid the notion of idol that is the fruit of Christian interpretation, all the more so as we know, at least for the Germanic peoples, that the pagans did not depict their gods. It was the numinous powers of the place that were worshipped, and one penitential says that these practices occurred "for the veneration of the place" (*pro veneratione loci*)! Much earlier, Pliny the Elder wrote in his *Natural History:*

> Once upon a time trees were the temples of the deities, and in conformity with primitive ritual, simple country places even now dedicate a tree of exceptional height to a god.[5]

The use of the plural to put the term "gods" into a singular perspective will again be noted! According to Tacitus (*Germania,* chap. IX), the ancient Germans "judge it not in accord with the greatness of the gods to confine them with walls or to liken them in appearance to any human countenance. They consecrate woods and groves."[6]

There are a great many parallels in classical antiquity. The Pelaspians worshipped numinous powers in the forest of Dodona. Numerous Greek temples had their own sacred grove and, we are told by Claudius Aelianus, the person who cut down even the smallest tree therein would be condemned to death. The Romans had their sacred service tree surrounded by a wall at the foot of the Palatine Hill. Not far from Rome, the Laurentians worshipped a wild olive tree that Virgil dubbed with a revealing name: "Faun of the Laurentians." Cato the Elder tells us that before cutting trees, it is necessary to make a sacrifice and say a prayer beginning with: "If you are god or goddess . . ." This immediately brings to mind the verse by Ronsard:

> *Stay, woodsman, stay thy hand awhile, and hark—*
> *It is not trees that thou art laying low!*
> *Dost thou not see the dripping life-blood flow*
> *From Nymphs that lived beneath the rigid bark?*
> *Unholy murderer of our Goddesses.*
> *If for some petty theft a varlet hangs,*
> *What deaths hast thou deserved, what bitter pangs,*
> *What brandings, burnings, tortures, dire distress!*[7]

The indeterminacy of the phrase recorded by Cato shows that it was a supernatural power, an as-yet-nameless entity that was being addressed. According to Thietmar of Merseburg, the pagan temple of Radegost (Rethra) was surrounded by a "vast forest, intact and venerable." Around 1008, Wigbert destroyed the sanctuary of Zutibure (*svetibor* means "sacred wood") and built a church on its site. The Venerable Bede tells how Coifi, the pagan priest of King Edwin of Northumbria, destroyed the local sanctuary. "He commanded his companions to destroy the temple with all its hedges" (*destruere fanum cum omnibus septis*). This site next took the name of Godmundingham, "home of the protectors of God."[8]

Objections could be raised that there are extant accounts that run counter my hypothesis that the word "idol" in fact covers a local *numen* that is not necessarily depicted. Let us take a look at them. According to Gregory of Tours, Clotilde told Clovis: "They are nothing, those gods you worship. . . . They are in fact carved in any kind of stone, wood, or metal." This general observation proves nothing because it derives directly from the third commandment (Deuteronomy 5:8–9): "Thou shalt not make thee any graven image, or any likeness of any thing. . . . Thou shalt not bow down thyself unto them, nor serve them." Clotilde quoted these words in an attempt to convert her husband. We do not have statues of deities from before the Roman era, and the first depictions are of foreign manufacture.

Today we assume these autochthonous "idols" were probably made in imitation. It has been long maintained that the ancient Germans were reluctant to depict their gods, and trees or posts, sometimes carved with a human head, served as images of the higher powers.* Incidentally, I would like to point out that Irminsul, the cosmic tree or pillar (*axis mundi*), is glossed in Latin texts as *fanum* and *idolum*, "sanctuary" and "idol," which is hardly precise.

Of greater interest is the *Vita S. Galli* (Life of Saint Gallus), written between 816 and 824 by Wetti of Reichenau.[9] Gallus and Colomban came to Brigantia (Bregenz), at the end of Lake Constance, where "the superstitious pagans worshipped three statues of copper and gold." Walafrid Strabo (died 849) specifies that these "bronze images [were] fixed to the walls" of a temple. Jacob Grimm compared this to a passage from Zosimus's account (after 439) of the idol of Athanaric, the *armamaxa,* which the Goths paraded on a chariot, but rightly pointed out that the three statues in Bregenz were located in the chapel dedicated to Saint Aurelia. Laurentius Knappert has shown with some likelihood that the *tres imagines* are in fact those of mother-goddesses.[10]

Without reiterating his argument (with which I am in agreement),

---

*In Norse texts such a depiction is called a *trémaðr,* a "tree-man" or "wooden man."

I will note that these deities are directly linked to the local land, and so intimately that if we rely on the epigraphy and research cited earlier by Siegfried Gutenbrunner, we can quite easily see in them individualized local spirits, *numens* given a name and who have a connection with the place they are protecting. If one rejects this argument, then we need reconsider the fact that "worship of the mother-goddesses never banished the worship of local guardian spirits," as Laurentius Knappert noted about the work of M. von Wal.[11] It is precisely in the same region where we find monuments of the *matres* that traces remain from the worship of local land spirits. An inscription found near Xanten tells us that Septimus Flavius Severus founded a temple with trees for the *Matres Quadruburgenses* and the genius loci.[12] According to another inscription, Caius Tauricius Verus fulfilled his oath "to all the gods and all the goddesses, to the *deae Vapthiae* and to the genius loci":

> *In h. d. d. deab(us)q. omnib(us) Matribus Vapthiabus et Genio loco sacrum*
>
>   *C. Tauricius Verus bf. Cos. Pro se et suis v.s.l.m. posuit et dedi(cavit)*[13]

On many inscriptions we find the spirits combined with gods, like to the *Matrae Suleis* (CIL 13, 31171), to Silvanus and Diana (CIL 13, 8492), and to the *Ambiomarc(i)ae* (CIL 13, 7789). Elsewhere we see names that could be those of female land spirits. The Alaferhuiae are designated as "nymphs" (CIL 13, 7862), and Lobbo is called *genius* on stone tablets found in Utrecht.

Other gods would seem to fall into the category of household spirits rather than that of land spirits. This is the case with the *Matres Aufaniae* (CIL 13, 8021), who, on an *ex-voto* of L. Maiorus Cogitatus, are combined with the guardian land spirits, *tutelae loci* (CIL 13, 6665), although the *fania* element of the name is assumed to have the meaning "swamp" (as in English "fen"). Some inscriptions reflect elements of the landscape, such as *Sulevia* with regard to the mountain (CIL 3,

1601 and 2, 1181), and the *Junoniae* (CIL 13, 8612) became, as we know, fairies in the Middle Ages, as did the *Campestres* (CIL 7, 1084). A more extensive investigation would undoubtedly turn up further confirmations.

It is, of course, quite difficult to form a more definitive judgment because the information is too laconic and rare, but I believe what we are faced with here is an amalgam, one all the easier to achieve in that time as first the Romans and then the Church used their own terms and concepts to describe and absorb the indigenous beliefs.

Moreover, the borders are blurred between natural creatures, the small spirits of folk mythology, and—since the major pagan gods were no longer actively worshipped—those beings that are hidden behind the names of Jupiter (Thor, Donar), Mercury (Odin), and Neptune. We do not know if what we see involves the elevation of a spirit to the rank of a god or the downgrading of a god into a demon (in the Greek sense of the word), or again the individualization of the hypostasis of a member of the pagan pantheon. The convergence between mother-goddesses and local land spirits could quite simply be the result of the syncretism of different forms of one and the same belief. The study of place-names can add some elements to help us evaluate all these facts.

7

The Evidence
of Place-Names

It is common knowledge that pagans named a large number of places after their gods, but Christians did the same with the saints and a study of the map of a recently colonized country, such as Canada, reveals how the appropriation of a piece of land occurs: it is placed under the patronage of a saint.

The whole of the medieval West is teeming with theophoric names. Here are a few examples: *Lugdunum* (France, Lyon) from Lugh, the well-known Celtic god; *Odensakr* (Norway) "Odin's Field"; *Froyle* (England), constructed from Fro/Freyr, Germanic god of the third function (fertility/fecundity); *Narvik* (Norway), "Njord's Bay," named after the god who is the father of Freya and Freyr. In short, we can find as many names of this sort as we can find places today named after Saint Martin, Saint Dennis, or Saint Michael. Thanks to philology, we now know that Oslo means "Sacred grove of the Aesir" (*Aslundr*), and that *Lugdunum* means "Hill of the god Lugh." But some names do not reflect the physical geography, nor high mythology, nor Christianity. They do not derive from family names, nor do they commemorate some event. Here is where things start to become interesting.

In order to narrow the focus, I have chosen German place-names as

47

references because, given the extent of the data to analyze, it is unthinkable to try to take into account all the toponyms of Western Europe. This would be akin to trying to fill the water jar of the Danaides! What all these place-names can reveal confirms what the texts say.

Alongside names that are self-explanatory such as *Heilighberc* ("Sacred Mountain," attested in 816), *Heiligbrunno* ("Sacred Spring/Fountain," attested 823), *Heiligenforst* ("Sacred Forest," ca. 1065), or *Sacrum nemus* ("Sacred Grove," eleventh century), we find others in which a physical element is connected with a spirit or demon. Although less numerous, names like this include *Scratinpach* (eighth century) and *Scratinberge* (1120), which mean "Schrat's Stream" and "Schrat's Mountain," respectively (the *Schrat* is a creature that has been made into a dwarf but is comparable, all in all, to the Weeper of the Jura region). A Thurse is a giant of Germanic mythology and we similarly find *Thursinruth,* the "Clearing of the *Thurse,*" and *Turssental* (1131) and *Tursinberch* (1158), the "Vale" and the "Mount" of the T(h)urse, respectively. There is *Wihtungen* that can be translated as "the Dwarves," with the understanding that *wiht* is an all-purpose word used to designate supernatural creatures whose name one dares not speak aloud. The devotion given to stones is attested by the place-name *Wihestaine* (twelfth century), the "sacred" or "consecrated stones"; and likewise for forests with *Wihinloh* (901), streams and rivers with *Wigbeke* (1007), and the mountains with *Wihenberc* (in all these place-names, the first element *wih/wig* means "to make sacred, to sanctify"). From a name like *Wichtlisperc* (1111) we can infer that the mountain in question was reputedly inhabited by creatures related to dwarves, a *wihtlin* (little wight) being synonymous with a *zwerc* (dwarf).

In the British Isles we find the place-names *Puclan cyrce* (946), "Pucel's Church"; *Pokin Tuna* (1201), "Puck's Yard"; and *Pokerich* (1314), "Puck's Stream." Puck, diminutive form *Pucel* (the Norse *puki* and the German *puk*), can refer to a revenant as well as a demon and a dwarf, but its meaning stabilized around the eleventh century and became consistent with that of "dwarf." Shakespeare features a certain Puck by the side of Oberon in his *A Midsummer Night's Dream*. In Scandinavia, a close look at the sagas gives us place-names like *Tröllaskogr,* "Forest of the Trolls"; *Trollahals,* "Troll Ridge"; *Trollaskeid,* "Path of the Trolls"; and in the Shetland Isles we find *Thursasker,* "Reef of the Thurse." In France, the toponymy of the Franche-Comté region carries traces of Guyon, the name of an evil spirit connected with boulders who may be identical with the Celtic Gwyllion.

Although they may not be as common, it is readily apparent that these names are quite comparable to those found in French localities that reveal dracs, fairies, and ladies, especially near springs and fountains. Local land spirits have left many traces, such as in Belgium where the most common representatives are the Lutôn and the Duhôn, which can be traced back to an ancient Gallic divine entity named Dusios. The Breton spirit called a *tuz,* diminutive form *tuzik,* is also related to Dusios.

The evidence from ancient names is quite scarce for three reasons: the Romans rebaptized local spirits with names coming from their culture; the Church often substituted the names of the saints for the older names; and the studies of place-names are essentially devoted to finding the names of gods and therefore don't focus attention on the place-names that refer to other creatures. We will now leave the Germanic-Scandinavian area for the Roman world, and to do so, let us consider the case of Silvanus, who was Christianized as Saint Silvanus (Sylvain in French).

8

Silvanus and Company

Silvanus is an extraordinary field of research that remains largely untilled, so I can present here some very broad lines that others, it is to be hoped, will develop more extensively.[1]

Silvanus is regarded as the spirit of the fields and flocks, forests and plantations (*Silvanus agrestis*), as well as the guardian of boundaries (*Silvanus orientalis*) and homes (*Silvanus domesticus*). According to the fragments of a Roman surveyor's journal, the Silvanus orientalis was placed at the edge of the fields, in a sacred grove (*in confinio lucus positus*). He was given the title "salutary" (*salutaris*) because he was considered a benefactor. Etymologically speaking, he is a spirit of the forests (*silva*) and even, probably, their numen, as the Indo-European suffix *-no,* which is part of the name, implies sovereignty.*

First and foremost, then, Silvanus means "Master of the Forest." This is what Stacius and Servius claim. According to Horace, offerings of milk and fruit were given to him. Today it is accepted that Silvanus was a spirit of the wooded land bordering on clearings. We know he had a temple on the Aventine Hill in Rome, and another near the Viminal Hill. A great number of altars dedicated to him have been discovered,

---

*A Germanic example of this suffix is *–nir,* which can be seen in *Jólnir,* a byname of Odin meaning "Master of *Jól,*" the name of the pagan Yuletide.

but his true sanctuary is the forest and the devotion surrounding him came entirely from the common folk.

The variety of his functions are evident in the epithets that are attached to his name. While "holy," "unvanquished," "happy," "heavenly," "father," and "guardian" are all rather general, the compounds ending in *-fer* are eloquent. *Pecudifer, lactifer, glandifer, poncifer, cannabifer, linifer* mean, respectively, "He who encourages the reproduction of the flocks," "He who produces milk," "He who produces acorns, "He who produces fruits," "He who makes the hemp grow," and "He who makes the trees grow." This is an agrarian deity or spirit, and Isidore of Seville named him *rusticorum deus,* "god of the peasants" (*Etymologiae,* VIII, 11, 81). Lavedan, who provides a rich iconography of this figure, thinks that "the primitive kind of Sylvain was probably a tree or stump. Pliny informs us that this was the case with the image of the god erected beneath a fig tree in front of the Temple of Saturn."[2]

Silvanus followed the Roman army in its conquests and by virtue of his wild (or rustic and silvicultural) nature he assimilated the local spirits and even the gods. We know, for example, that he was integrated with Sucellus, the god of the mallet. He did not banish the indigenous deities but coexisted with them, which is often indicated in the label affixed to him and which connects him to a specific place. We find a *Silvanus Poeninus* in Tirnovo (Bulgaria), a *Silvanus Cocidius* near Hadrian's Wall in Britain, and a *Silvanus Sinquatis* in Géromont (Belgium). In Spain we see a *Silvanus Caldouelicos* who guards hot springs.

The spread of Silvanus's popularity in the following period is attested by Christian anthroponomastics. According to the Benedictines of Paris, who compiled lives of the saints, there were nineteen named Sylvain (Silvain) and four named Sylvester, whose commemoration corresponded with carnival-related times of the year (February, May, August, November, and year's end). The feast day of Saint Sylvester falls on December 31. Is it mere coincidence that this date was once one on which men disguised themselves in costume as wild animals, which was violently condemned by preachers?[3]

In turn, the saints gave their names to human settlements, a process that may have been encouraged by the local presence of a spirit that had already been merged with Silvanus. In France this gives us Saint-Silvain in the Calvados, Corrèze, Creuse, and Maine-et-Loire regions; a Saint-Sauvant in Charente-Inférieur; a Saint-Sauvent in Vienne; a Saint-Sauves in Puy-de-Dôme; a Souvignardes (*Silvinianicus*) in the Gard; and a Sauvagnon (*Sylvanius*) in the lower Pyrenees.

Thus when we encounter names like silvanus, faunus, pilosus, and so on in medieval Latin texts, it is essential to remember that most of the time these are concealing local spirits. Below are some examples. Here is what Burchard of Worms wrote in his Decretum around 1010:

> Hast thou made little child's bows and child's shoes, and hast thou cast them into thy storeroom or thy barn, so that *satyrs* and *fauns* [my italics] might play with them in this very place in order that they might bring to thee the goods of others so that thou shouldst be made rich?[4]

Notker the Stammerer speaks of a Hairy One (pilosus) that haunts a forge, but he also calls it a Larva. At the beginning of the thirteenth century, Gervase of Tilbury wrote:

> Many are those who, in their own experience, have seen Silvains, that are called incubi and which the French call Duses (*Dusii*), and Pans.[5]

What we have seen regarding Silvanus can be extended to other rustic female creatures who are simply called *agrestes foeminae, sylvaticae,* and *Matres Campestres,* a definition encompassing nymphs, dryads, Diana, and Dictynne, as well as indigenous spirits.[6] In Germany, *sylvatica* is regularly translated as "woman of the wood" (*holzwîp*), and dryad by "weeper of the wood" (*holzmuowa*). Diana and Dictynne were grouped together under the generic term of *agrestes foeminae,* which corresponds to the locution "wild women" in Middle High German. Glosses and translations indicate that in many cases indigenous elements matched those that came from the Roman world.

In fact, all the information strongly points to a single truth: regardless of the people and the time period in question, the world is peopled by creatures that bear many different names. In short, the great god Pan is not as dead as has been claimed!

9

The Metamorphoses of Spirits

It should be clear that we need to spend a bit more time looking at the names of all these spirits and, even more importantly, we should focus on the notion of amalgamation. Many scholars and researchers have attempted, more or less successfully, to identify the local land spirits and demons that are concealed beneath the cover terms and generic terms we've just been discussing, and they have tried to get a clear view of the relations woven over the course of centuries between these spirits and the dead, the dwarves, the giants, and even the saints. These problems, which are crucial because they limit our understanding of earlier mindsets, need to be elucidated, so here I will develop a bit further what I have merely sketched out in previous studies.

We can state immediately that the Latin-Roman terminology used by clerics did irreparable damage to local beliefs. Clerics in fact substituted southern "equivalents" for the indigenous names, and the vernacular writers further advanced this process by using a reduced lexicon in which the terms "dwarves" and "giants" held the greatest importance. In the Roman sphere we know that "dwarf" can also mean a sprite, goblin, changeling, Duse, household spirit, a Narove, or even certain categories of wild men, simply because these creatures have been leveled with one another linguistically.

In the first stage, they received the Latin names of Roman land spirits (*faunus, pilosus, satyrus, panes,* and so on); in the second stage, only the features they shared in common were retained. For example, these beings could conceal themselves easily in wild places, they were reputed to be small in size (which is completely false as they could change size at will), they possessed supernatural powers, and they could bestow prosperity or misfortune. The *interpretatio romana* hides many things, of course, but the regularity with which it was applied makes it apparent that it masks something else. There is one clue that offers a glimpse of what this might be: the authors who wrote in Latin were uncomfortable when dealing with local beliefs and they often used at least two terms to render something that had one name in the vernacular.

Several lengthy studies conducted with regard to the Germanic elements allow me to say that dwarf (*zwerc*), for example, can designate a tormented soul as well as an elf, a nightmare (perceived as an evil spirit), a kobold, and other household spirits.[1] The shift in meaning between dwarves and spirits is explained by the fact that they share the same habitat. Both mythology as well as German folk beliefs indicate that dwarves dwell in the stones, or beneath them. It so happens that these places are also home to elves and tutelary spirits. Here are two examples. In the *Ynglinga saga* (Saga of the Ynglings) it is described how one day when King Sveigðir was returning from a drinking bout, he saw a dwarf seated at the foot of a stone, who invited the king to follow him; they both entered the stone, and the king never returned. In the *Þáttr Þorvalds ens Víðförla* (Tale of Thorvald Far-Traveler), a stone stands in Gilja to which the parents of Kodran made sacrifices and where they claimed their tutelary spirit, the guardian of their estate, lived.

As both land and household spirits are regularly called *pilosus* or *satyrus* (as claimed by Burchard of Worms), and both terms are consistently glossed or translated by "dwarf" in the Germanic linguistic area, they became dwarves and lost a great many of their unique features.

The following table, created from Middle High German glossaries and lexicons, offers an excellent glimpse of the amalgams that took place:

pilosus		*incubus/succubus*
wiht		*silenus/silvanus*
schrat		*fanus/panes*
pilwiz	—>*zwerc* = *schrat*<—	*larva*
pumilio		*penates*
nanus/pygmaeus		*satyrus*

It can be easily seen that the "dwarf" (*zwerc*) or *schrat* have assimilated and subsumed a variety of very different creatures, which is the reason for the difficulty affecting all studies of this subject.

In the Germanic-Scandinavian realm, local land spirits are called *landvættir* (plural), but they are often commingled with elves (*álfar*), giants (thurses and trolls), and even with the dead as well as with the *Dísir*,[2] ancient deities of the third function.* In recent times in Iceland it was still believed that the "Stones of the Land Dísir" (*Landdísarsteinar*) were the home of the genii loci.

These land spirits were merged with elves since the latter had also been confused with dwarves and therefore lost, long before the year 1000, their nature as helpful beings. It should not be forgotten that elves were worshipped. Prayers and sacrifices were offered to them in exactly the same way as to local spirits. The Church demonized elves for this reason by making them into malevolent and deadly dwarves and emanations of Satan, as I have shown before. They are confused with the giants who live in wild areas, and with the dead who spend their lives beyond the grave inside the mountains.

The "dweller in the mountain" (*bergbúi*) is for this reason sometimes a dead soul and sometimes a giant. All of these beings were

---

*[According to the categorizations of the comparative mythologist Georges Dumézil, Indo-European religion and social structure was marked by a tripartite division: the "first function" concerned sovereignty and magic, the "second function" concerned war and defense, and the "third function" concerned fertility and production. —*Trans.*]

commingled in a process of collective anathematization and became demons. A runic staff from Bergen (Norway), which could date from 1200, offers evidence of these depreciations:

> *I carve the runes of remedy,*
> *I carve the runes of protection,*
> *Once against the elves,*
> *Twice against the trolls,*
> *Thrice against the thurses.*

A curse that is recounted in the *Bósa saga ok Herrauðs* (Saga of Bósi and Herraud), which probably dates from earlier than the twelfth century, says:

> *May trolls and elves*
> *and wizard-norns,*
> *the dwellers [of holes, rocks, and so on]*
> *and the giants of the mountains (bergrisar)*
> *burn your hall.*
> *May the frost thurses rend you!*[3]

These two texts provide a good glimpse of the individuals haunting the world of this period. In the third verse, the plural "dwellers" (*búar*) is a collective noun designating all the spirits (Norse *vættir;* Middle High German *wihte*) inhabiting nature. Moreover, the Bergen amulet and the saga are useful in showing us the merger that took place between different creatures that the Church simply designated with the cover term *troll*, which came to mean "demon" and "devil."

The merging of land spirits and giants seem to have occurred fairly simply: while the Frost Giants (*hrímþursar*) live far away in their own world (*Jötunheimr*), the Mountain Giants (*bergrisar*) live close to human habitations. One text reveals how they could behave like veritable genii loci:

According to the *Book of Settlements,* one night Björn dreamed that a dweller of the mountains (*bergbúi*) came to him and offered to partner with him, and he accepted that offer. After that, a strange billy goat came to join his herds, and his livestock multiplied so rapidly that he soon became rich. He was nicknamed Billy-goat Björn (*Hafr-Björn*). People gifted with second sight could see that the guardian spirits of the land (*landvættir*) accompanied Björn to the assembly, and Thorsteinn and Thordr [his brothers] when they hunted and fished.[4]

Now that this point has been clarified, let us consider the merger made between the spirits and the dead. When a man was remembered well after his death, when his life was beneficial to the community, he enjoyed for a short time after his departure a particular status: the pagans made him a god or spirit, the Christians a saint, but the reaction is the same. In his history of the Norse kings, *Heimskringla,* Snorri Sturluson cites Frey, king of the Swedes (*Svíar*), whose rule was marked by prosperity and peace. "They . . . called him the God of the World and sacrificed to him ever after for good harvests and peace."[5] The same was true for Halfdan the Black, whose corpse was cut into pieces and each piece buried beneath a mound in each province; the *Flateyjarbók* (I, 537) adds: "Many folk made sacrifices to these mounds."

Exactly the same thing happens with with the bodies of saints. They are dismembered and the pieces are placed into reliquaries that are then housed in churches. Pierre-André Sigal, who has studied these matters in depth, writes: "The proximity of the relics in fact creates the formation of a kind of sanctified zone in the form of a series of concentric circles, whose sacredness increases as you move from the periphery toward the center."[6] Dieter Harmening speaks in this regard of a "zone of concentration of the sacred": "When someone approaches a sanctuary, he crosses through a series of zones materialized by the place from where the sanctuary becomes visible, the church cemetery, the threshold, and so forth."[7] We should note that some pilgrims could not cross over the threshold because they were halted by a supernatural force, and this revealed their sinful status. In French-speaking areas the *aître* (*atrium*), whose border corresponds with the cemetery, was a defensive boundary, and those who crossed it with hostile feelings were chastised by the local numen, as can be read in the *Vita S. Urbani, episcopi Lingonen* (Life of Saint Urban, bishop of Langres).[8]

This manner of transforming the dead into numinous powers is not reserved to Christianity, mythological texts, or fiction. The historical Icelandic *Book of Settlements* provides the following information:

> Because of his popularity, sacrifices were offered to Grim once he was dead and he was nicknamed *kambann*. (H 19)

One detail reveals that a man venerated in this way was not an ordinary deceased individual: "Einar lived in Laugarbrekka; he was buried beneath a tumulus . . . and his mound is always green, in winter and summer alike" (S 75). Thanks to the *Gísla saga Súrssonar* (Saga of Gisli Súrsson), we learn what this means. Thorgrim's tumulus remains green: "The people thought that their offerings had attracted the good graces of the god Freyr who did not want him to be cold" (chap. 18). In the *Ketils saga hœngs* (Saga of Ketil Hœngr) sacrifices are mentioned being made to a mound that the snow never covers (chap. 5).

The good dead individual therefore becomes, among other things, a conduit between the living and the higher powers. Such deification is a theme that can be found in the first chapter of the *Hervarar saga ok Heiðreks* (Saga of Hervör and Heidrek) and in the *Bárðar saga Snæfellsáss* (Saga of Bárðr Snæfellsáss). The details given in the latter text make it quite interesting; when Bard vanished, it was believed he had gone into the Mountain of the Snows—the inside of mountains is one form of the beyond—and prayers were made to him as if he were a god (*heitguð*). He was called "mountain spirit" (*bjargvættr*) and is nicknamed the "God of the Snaefell" (*Snaefellsáss*). It should be noted that a figure deified in this manner is intrinsically linked to a specific place.

Christianity offers similar examples of the spontaneous development of cults around the tombs of completely unknown individuals, and Pierre-André Sigal cites the examples of Saint Crescence (Paris), Saint Genès of Auvergne (Thiers), Saint Bénigne (Dijon), Saint Gui (Anderlecht), and Saint Godelième (Ghistelles).[9] In every instance an extraordinary or unusual event provided the evidence of the unique nature of the individual buried at that site. In the *Miracles de saint Paul, saint Clair et saint Quiriace,* written at the end of the twelfth century, mysterious lights appeared around a ruined chapel at the top of a hill. Those who behaved in a shameless manner there were quickly punished and these punishments even affected livestock.[10]

Such manifestations indicate that the place has been sanctified by the body of the deceased, and the reaction of both pagans and Christians when confronted by such an event is basically identical: a cult is formed. Beyond all differences due to era, country, or religion, beliefs are born and evolve in the same way.

If one refers to the texts, it is undeniably clear that the dead individual becomes a tutelary spirit of a specific location. In the Celtic sphere, the *Triads* in the medieval Welsh manuscript *Llyfr Coch Hergest* (Red Book of Hergest) say that the head of Llyr's son, Bran the Blessed, was hidden in the White Hill of London with its head turned facing France. As long as it remained in that position, the Saxons could not oppress the island. The remains of Gwerthefyr (*Guorthemir*) the Blessed were hidden in the principal ports of this island and so long as they remained concealed there was no fear the Saxons would invade the country.[11] Pomponius Mela tells how the Philaeni brothers had themselves buried beneath a dune to ensure Carthage took possession of a contested territory and, certainly, in order to become tutelary spirits. The place took the name of Arae Philaenorum.

It is safe to say that after a certain stretch of time nothing remains of the good dead individual except his aspect as a spirit. Time eventually banishes his name and deeds from memory. Later there occurs a merging between local spirits and the deceased. This type of merger is still detectable in Scandinavian folk beliefs collected in the nineteenth century. One legend records the following: a peasant gave offense to a genius loci (*gardvord,* literally a "guardian of the estate") and the narrator of the tale remarks: "He should not have done so because the *gardvord* is the soul (or the spirit or ghost: *attrgangaren*) of the man that cleared that land where the house stands, so he should be honored and respected."[12]

The dispute that has been and continues to be argued over between some researchers about whether the spirit came before the dead individual or vice versa is baseless and rests on a partial vision of the facts. It is excusable because a great deal of time must be devoted to these studies before the fog that so thickly surrounds this complex of beliefs begins to dissipate. In fact the good dead and the spirits were distinct from one another originally. They were gradually merged together, and then combined with other creatures.

This amalgam came about on two levels, in my opinion: 1) the local spirits and the dead worthy of offerings were merged with elves by virtue of the latter's beneficial nature and their habitat; 2) all were the object of agrarian and/or domestic worship, and they were therefore demonized by the Church and merged with the dwarves, creatures reputedly malevolent and dreadful. Since these creatures also lived in the natural wild, it was easy for churchmen toiling for the greater glory of God (*ad maioram Dei Gloriam!*) to incorporate them with spirits, if only by virtue of the Augustinian principle according to which pagans worshipped demons. This shift in meaning—which was a brilliant move because it played upon an already existing opposition among the indigenous people between spirits/the dead/beneficial elves, and malefic dwarves—was quite prominent in the national lexicons of the Middle Ages, especially in the Germanic lands where the scribes were indifferent in their use of the names corresponding to elf, dwarf, and spirit. An example of this drift is provided by *alp* (elf), which became the name of the nightmare, a substitution that speaks for itself.

Although the evidence for it is much more sparse, it is not

impermissible to think that these mergers were also facilitated by the lumping together of the dangerous dead and evil spirits (*meinvættir*). If the good deceased became a good spirit, why couldn't the evil deceased—someone whose death took place under strange circumstances, or who had been a wizard, seer, or who had been a terror to his neighbors because of his asocial and brutal nature—become a demon? A passage from the Icelandic *Book of Settlements* deserves our attention:

> Ölvir, son of Eysteinn, took the land east of the Grimsá. No one had dared settle this area because of the land spirits since the time Hjörleif had been slain. (S 330)

It so happens that Hjörleif had been treacherously murdered by his slaves, which means, according to the thinking of the ancient Scandinavians, that he had the right to avenge himself and thus return from the grave. Another hypothesis is conceivable: he had made an alliance with the land spirits of the area in which he settled, and they would not accept intruders. A second clue corroborates the fact that the evil dead are dangerous. People got rid of their corpses by burying them in remote locations, far from the passage of men and livestock. This is what was done with the body of Thorolf Halt-Foot in the *Eyrbyggja Saga,* and the danger that such corpses pose is often indicated in the place-name. The place where Olaf Tryggvason had sorcerers drowned was called *Skrattasker,* "Sorcerers' Reef," but *skratti,* which we encountered above in its German form *schrat,* also designates malevolent spirits that live in the wild. The place where Hallbjörn Whetstone-Eye was buried is called *Skrattavardi,* "Sorcerers' Cairn."[13]

The assimilation of the dangerous dead and malevolent spirits clearly emerges from the place-names cited above. It must also be conceded that spirits are not only neutral or benevolent. The Norse designate these evil spirits by the word *meinvættir,* and a passage from the *Grettis saga Ásmundarsonar* (Grettir's Saga) is eloquent in this regard:

Thorhall lived in Thorhallsstadir in Forsaeludal, inland from Vatnsdale. He had trouble finding shepherds because the place was haunted. He managed to hire Glam, a ferocious Swede, but he failed to return in the evening, as was his habit, on Christmas night. The next day a search was made for him, the sheep were found scattered about as well as traces of giant footsteps. The searchers reached a place where a savage struggle had taken place, the earth was trampled, many rocks had been torn up, and large spots of blood were seen on the ground. Glam's corpse lay a bit farther on. The men returned and told Thorhall that the evil spirit (*meinvættr*) that had long lurked there must have slain Glam.[14]

It should not be forgotten that the deceased are never truly dead and can take action from their graves. Saxo Grammaticus tells of the setbacks suffered by those who tried to violate Baldr's tumulus. The guardian spirits of the site struck them with terror and sent them fleeing. When they finally managed to open the tomb, a torrent of water gushed out. In his analysis of this passage, Paul Hermann pointed out that the deceased was behaving both as a spirit and a mound-dweller (*haugbúi*).[15]

In the saga bearing his name, Hervör asks that a stop be made at the Isle of Samsey where warriors were buried beneath the mounds, but his companions opposed him saying that "large evil spirits" (*miklar meinvættir*) walked there day and night (chap. 4). Even at the beginning of the twentieth century, the Swedish Lapps (Sámi) avoided erecting their tents over spots where death had occurred for fear of disturbing the sleep of the dead or prompting their vengeance, as the spirits of the dead were believed to settle in these spots.[16] This precaution was all the more justified as the dead had long been buried on mountains and in forests, even though cemeteries had come into general use since around 1641.

Among other things, it was thought that disturbing the dead incurred the risk of causing them to send illnesses. In Norway, if someone falls ill after sleeping in a field or deserted forest, people say that he slept too close to the spirits. He should return to that spot and ask forgiveness.[17] It is important to realize, however, that even the most civilized areas are not immune to such attacks. Legend claims that an individual named Kairik fell asleep on a bench in the Gällivare church and its land spirits—in this case, the dead buried in the church—made him ill. In fifteenth-century Germany, dangerous areas were called *unsteten* (singular: *unstete*), which were described as being "places of uncertainty" (*loca incerta*). "When someone who walks there is struck by a sudden illness or feel pains in his limbs, the ignorant say: 'He has gone over an *unstete*.'" It is claimed that the land spirit has punished him for having violated its sanctity (*et quia is sanctus sit, genius loci illum punisse*).[18]

10

A Provisional Assessment

The reader now has all the elements necessary for evaluating and understanding the facts, which can be summarized as follows. The giants, dwarves, and dragons of romances and hagiographical legends can conceal local land spirits. The latter are complex figures—the emanations of natural forces or the dead. The Medieval Latin texts need to be read closely to discover that *incubi* and *larvae,* for example, are not always what their authors claim. A word like "idol" overlies another reality and the remnants of worship are not directed solely at the great gods. Spirits existed before the established religions.

Our world is haunted and inhabited, even if it is only rarely or by chance that we recognize our neighbors. Civilization has repressed some into deserted solitudes, impenetrable forests, and inaccessible mountains. In his travel account known as *Rihla* (The Journey), the Moroccan explorer Ibn Battûta (1304–1368/9) wondered whether the dwellers in the "Land of Darkness" (Scythia) were men or spirits.[1] Marco Polo tells us that spirits live in the Lop Desert and seek to slay men through illusions (mirages?).[2]

Yet other "spirits" have stayed in place, mainly near springs and wells. But they are small in number with most fleeing human beings and keeping their distance. Depending upon the location and the time period, they can be found under a wide variety of names throughout the entire West and even elsewhere, both in the Middle Ages and more recently, and what has been recorded of them has scarcely changed over the centuries. They represent the continued existence of ancestral beliefs, and they materialize fears and desires and the need to explain incomprehensible and alarming phenomena. To a certain extent, they symbolize man's struggle against an as yet untamed nature.

For the individual seeking to settle on a virgin piece of ground, there are three available options: defeat the numinous powers, come to terms with them, or surrender the land to them. We shall now turn our attention to this situation.

PART TWO

Conquering and Defending the Land

The ruling demon of the Perilous Vale.
Illustration from The Travels of John
Mandeville. *Augsburg: Anton Sorg, 1480.*

11
Encountering the Spirits of the Local Land

In classical antiquity as well as in the Middle Ages, the virgin spaces that people wished to settle upon prompted prudence. Every colonization, settlement, and addition of a place to the civilized domain was therefore accompanied by rites that conferred a different sanctity to the space being appropriated and gave its owner legitimacy. If these rites were not heeded, the inhabitants of the place in question would treat the newcomers as intruders and threaten their livelihood, their mental health, and even their lives. Furthermore, the conquest was never definitive and whenever a farm, hamlet, temple, chapel, or castle was abandoned, it fell back into the power of the local land spirits.

The secular texts do not tell us a great deal about encounters with local land spirits, and in fact the most eloquent accounts of these meetings are found in the lives of the saints. Hrosvitha tells us, for example, that Gandersheim Convent was built "in a sylvan area full of fauns and phantoms"—we now know what to make of these terms—where many will o' the wisps appeared.[1]

Gregory of Tours recorded the following in his *Vita Patrum* (Life of the Fathers). When Lupicinus and Romanus reached the solitary retreats of the Jura and settled there, they found themselves under attack from demons.

> In fact, the demons did not stop hitting them with stones for even a day. Each time they bent their knees to pray to the Lord, a rain of pebbles thrown by the demons immediately rained down upon them.[2]

In the *Vita S. Romani* (Life of Saint Romanus), written around 520, there is one passage that grabs our attention. Sabinianus had settled in the valley by the bank of a river—probably the Tacon—at the foot of the butte on which stood the Condat Monastery:

> The devil attacked him. Every night without relief he tormented him with such unleashed fury that he was not granted even an instant of sleep. Because, in addition to the repeated impacts on the walls, his poor roof was destroyed in a loud clamor of stones.[3]

The *Life of Saint Gallus,* written by Wetti in the ninth century, is worth examining because it recounts the apostle's attempt to settle in a wild and pagan region:

> Between 561 and 575, Gallus, accompanied by his deacon Hiltibodus, arrived in Pregnetia, Bregenz by Lake Constance, where "superstitious pagans worshipped three gold and copper statues and prayed more to them than to the world's Creator." He preached, then "broke the images against the rocks and threw them into the deepest part of the lake, and some of the people were converted. A short time later in the silence of the night, while Gallus was washing his nets in the lake, he heard a "demon" calling from the mountaintops to another who was in the depths of the lake. "Help me," he cried, "strangers have come who have driven me from my temple."

The aquatic demon answered him: "One of them is now next to the lake but I cannot harm him and I have tried to destroy his nets in vain." Gallus signed himself and told everything to this abbot, who exorcised the demons. Then, a phantasmatic voice (*vox fantasmatica*) was heard from the heights, accompanied by moans and cries, "and the spirits vanished."

Implied here is that the local folk were addressing their prayers to the spirit of the mountain, in a temple that was in fact a former Christian sanctuary, according to the testimony of Ratpert in *Casus Sancti Galli*. This spirit is called the *pares* (peer) of the one in the water, which reflects a very clear notion. The natural elements are inhabited by beings of the same race, and Christianity drove them off, thus freeing sites whose legitimate inhabitants had been tamed, so to speak, by offerings or worship from the people who colonized the region. But let us pick up the story where we left off:

Still followed by Hiltibodus, Gallus built his hermitage in the solitary region on the banks of the Petrosa, the river teeming with fish that flowed into Lake Constance, near Rorschach. One day while fishing, Hiltibodus spotted two female "demons" who were throwing stones at him and bemoaning the death of the fish. They went on to say: "What are we to do? Because of this stranger, we can no longer remain among men, nor in solitude."

A little later, Hiltibodus was hunting and heard the spirits of Mount Himilinberc (Mountain of Heaven) mourning about the death in the neighborhood. A little later, Wetti notes that the pagans "falsely accused Saint Gallus to Duke Gunzo, saying that since the strangers arrived, game was scarce and hunting was poor" (*propter illos advenas venationes publicis in locis fuisse desolatas*).

Underneath the Christian overlay of the facts, a message is clear to read. The spirits of the land—women, when it concerns a body of water—and the spirits of the mountains are the legitimate owners of these places and the masters of the animals, which can be viewed as their herds. This becomes obvious if we refer to a group of legends that are very widespread in the Alps and concern a compulsive hunter who depopulates a region. The spirit of the place, who is also the master of its fauna, makes a pact with the hunter, promising to furnish all the game he needs as long as he refrains from hunting. One day the hunter surrendered to his hunting demon and was slain immediately. This legend was popularized in a famous ballad by Schiller.

This also explains a frequent theme in medieval writings that is especially well attested in the German regions: a hero kills an animal in the forest and is immediately confronted by a giant who demands compensation. The story known as *Virginal* or *Dietrichs erste Ausfahrt* (Dietrich's First Quest) provides an excellent illustration. Dietrich kills a wild boar in a grove and a giant looms up, asking who gave him permission to do that, and rushes at him. In *Yvain, the Knight of the Lion* by Chrétien de Troyes, the churl who guards the wild animals in a forest clearing and knows how to compel their obedience—they will slay any other person—should be regarded as the master of the beasts and thus a genius loci who has been disguised for the needs of the novel.

In hagiographic texts, the local land spirits most often take the form of monsters, but some details make it possible to see what they are disguising. Demonized, they turn into those dragons that the saints vanquish or drive away. A highly symbolic beast, the dragon represents paganism by virtue of something the Bible says—all that crawls is unclean (Leviticus 11:42)—but it is also the materialization of natural forces. When Krakow in Poland was founded, Graccus, the civilizing hero, had to slay a dragon that haunted Wawel Hill, and to do so he resorted to a ruse once used by Alexander the Great: he placed a bull full of poisonous substances near the beast's lair. Sometimes the monster lives at the border of the town and receives a sacrifice of men or animals every year until some holy man comes to put a stop to it. This is the case with the Graoully dragon that Saint Clement of Metz eliminated, the Lizard that Saint Quiriace drove away, the Gargoyle expelled by Saint Romanus of Rouen, and the victories of the Saint Loup over the Cocatrix and of Saint Véran over the Coulobre (from Latin *coluber* meaning "viper"). All these tales are part of the same complex. It will be noted that in each of these occasions the dragon is not slain but driven away, which clearly distinguishes these confrontations from that of Saint George and the dragon. Saint Véran drove the dragon from the Fountain of Vaucluse near Cavaillon and commanded it to disappear; the monster soared off toward the Alps and died at a spot that today bears the saint's name. In the legend of Saint Radegund (Poitiers), a dragon remains in the vicinity of the convent she founded, in a grotto by the banks of the Clain river. The beast is in the habit of carrying off the nuns to satisfy his hunger.

The expulsion of the dragon is a civilizing act and not only a Christian one. The threat it poses to humans is eliminated. In 1407, a three-headed, fire-breathing dragon lived on the banks of the Nive in the Bayonne region, devouring man and beast. Gaston Arnaut, a knight of Belzunce, confronted the monster. He slew it but was killed himself. The grateful populace thanked the Belzunce family with a gift of land.[4]

With great sagacity, Jacques Le Goff earlier showed how Saint Marcellus of Paris's victory over a dragon was the Christian form of man's victory over a genius loci. The *Vita S. Marcellini* (Life of Saint Marcellus) by Venantius Fortunatus, written around 575, contains one additional interesting detail: the emergence of a dragon is connected to the death of a matriarch of ill repute. The monster comes to devour the woman:

> Then the family members remaining in the neighborhood, hearing this noise, came rushing forward and saw an immense monster leaving the grave by unfurling its rings. . . . On learning what was happening, Saint Marcellus realized that he had to vanquish this bloodthirsty foe. . . . When the serpent left the forest to go to the grave, they walked toward each other. Saint Marcellus began to pray,

and the monster with his head down came to ask pardon with his caressing tail. Then Saint Marcellus struck his head *three times* with his cross, placed his stole around his neck, and displayed his triumph before the citizenry. . . . He then reprimanded the monster and told it: "Henceforth, *remain in the wilderness or hide in the water.*" The monster soon vanished, leaving no trace behind.[5]

I have italicized two important details that allow us to see the continuity of the underlying pagan thought. Furthermore, what stands out is the collusion between the evil dead woman and the emergence of the monster. The matriarch's sin opened a breech in the spiritual defenses of the area and allowed a dragon to enter. In a very interesting study conducted with great perspicacity, Raymond Delavigne has clearly shown how dragons are connected to flood-prone regions and this is where the highest concentration of dragon- or serpent-slaying saints are found.[6] He therefore confirms that the dragon is the Christian vision of a water spirit.

The legend of Saint Martha should be interpreted the same way:

When Martha arrived in the Aix region, she learned that in a wood between Arles and Avignon on the banks of the Rhone lived a dragon, half-reptile, half-fish, that slew any who passed by and sank ships. Martha found the dragon and cast holy water on it, and the monster became as calm as a lamb. Martha bound it with her belt, and the people slew it.

The dragon was called Tirascurus, hence the place took the name of Tirasconus; it had previously been called Nerluc, meaning Dark Wood, because of the somber groves it contained. It is easy to see that the beast had been forced back into the wild space lying in proximity to the town, which took the name of Tarascon and somehow forbid anyone from passing through its territory. Martha performed the task of a civilizer and expanded the world of humans by pushing out its boundaries, thus

giving new territories to man. Thanks to Louis Dumont's fine monograph on the Tarasque, we know that the processional dragons to whom
offerings were made are similar in nature to propitiatory rites intended
to attract fertility and prosperity to a community living in a specific
place.[7] The form taken by the intended recipient of these offerings,
whether it is monstrous or not, does not matter. What matters is that
this amounts to an attempt to conciliate the invisible powers, meaning
first and foremost the local land spirits.

Often the animal forms of land spirits come out when a saint
decided to settle in a place or finds himself there by chance. When
Saint Hilary landed on the isle of Gallinara (or the Isola d'Albenga), a
small island in the Ligurian Sea, it was full of snakes that fled when he
looked upon them. When William of Orange retired from the world, he
decided to establish his hermitage on a mountain in a deserted region,
but the place was teeming with "vermin."

> *The wilderness made the mountain a dreadful place*
> *Because of the large number of serpents there*
> *Adders and vipers and crested snakes*
> *And giant lizards and swollen ugly toads.*
> *In this desert did William come.* (*Le Moniage*
>   *Guillaume*, 2480–84)

In other cases, when men of God moved in, they repelled but did
not eliminate the figures representing natural forces or paganism. The
Roman du Mont-Saint-Michel by Guillaume de Saint-Pair appears like
the history of the Christianization of a site haunted by the presence
of pagan "deities." The *Miracles of Saint Eligius*,[8] written in Picardy
during the second half of the thirteenth century, even describes how a
troop of "devils" attacked a monastery:

> *Li diables a t'abeïe*
> *A nuit fierement envahïe.*

> *Tant ont venté, tant ont herlé,*
> *Que près que tout ont craventé*
> *Le fi Sathanus tout l'edifisse**

In *Morgant der Riese* (Morgant the Giant, a 1531 German adaptation of the romance *Il Morgante Maggiore* by Luigi Pulci), a monastery was founded in the wilderness but in close proximity "dwelled on the mountain three large, proud, and evil giants, who did great mischief to the monks by shooting enormous stones against their monastery with their slings" (chap. 4), and Roland was obliged to kill them to free the monks who were no longer even able to get water. With this text we find ourselves in a fictional realm that hardly differs from the hagiographical legends with regard to local land spirits. Out of the many pertinent examples, I have selected the story of Chapalu.

The *Vulgate Merlin* includes the story of the battle between King Arthur and the Lausanne cat known as Chapalu, a demonic monster that is connected to a sin, like the one in the *Life of Saint Marcellus*. Here is the story:

Merlin advised the king to go to the shores of Lake Geneva because his aid was needed there for the following reasons. Four years before, on Ascension Day, a sinful fisherman had gone out on the lake to fish. Before casting his net, he promised *our Lord the first fish he caught.* Thereupon the wicked man caught a splendid fish and decided to keep it for himself, reserving the second for God. He again caught a handsome fish on his second cast, but did not keep his promise. The third time he pulled from the water a little cat that was blacker than a Moor. He brought it home so it could catch rats and mice. The cat became monstrous and killed the fisherman, his wife, and their children:

---

*The devils invaded the abbey during the night. They created such strong gusts of wind and made such a clamor they destroyed almost everything, including the building, these spawn of Satan.

*Si le nori tant quil estrangla lui et sa femme et ses enfants, et puis s'enfuis en une montagne qui est outré le lac que je vous ai dit. Si a esté ilueques a ore si orchist et destruit quanqu'il ataint et il est a merveilles grans et expoentables.**

This place, Merlin adds, is located on the road to Rome where Arthur is planning to go, and if the king stops there, he will have the possibility of delivering people threatened with death by this monstrous cat, with the help of God. When Arthur and his barons heard this tale, they took fright and made the sign of the cross, clearly recognizing that this terrible beast was the punishment for a promise made to God and not kept. Arthur decided to go with his men to Lake Geneva. The king scaled the mountain accompanied by Loth, Gariet, Ban, and Merlin, who showed him the cat's lair. Arthur asked him what they needed to do to force the cat to leave its den and Merlin told him that he would see and that he should prepare himself for battle. The king sent his men away, wishing to take this task alone. Merlin imitated the cry of a wild animal, the famished cat rushed out and hurled itself upon Arthur, who slew it. After his victory, Arthur decided that this place, which hitherto had been called Mont dou Lac, would henceforth be known as Mont du Chat.[9]

Underneath its Christian trappings, the text is clear. Arthur's task is to rid the region of this scourge that a sin made possible. One of the characteristics that allows us to recognize the underlying presence of land spirits is the deserted nature of a piece of land. The hero or saint reestablishes divine order, pushing the demonic or ancestral forces a little farther back, or else eliminates them, providing humans with a territory they can cultivate and live upon. They are therefore perform-

---

*[He dutifully reared it until the day it strangled him, his wife, and his children, after which it fled into the mountain that was on the other side of the lake we spoke of earlier. It is still there to this day, and it will utterly kill and destroy anyone who chances upon it; it is incredibly huge and terrifying. —*Trans.*]

ing a civilizing task. On a mosaic in Otranto Cathedral, dating from the years 1163–1165, Arthur's battle with the Chapalu is depicted, but the king is riding an unidentified animal (possibly a goat) that is slain. André of Coutances in his *Li Romanz des Franceis,* written before 1204, also gives us this version of events.

Many questions have been raised about the Chapalu and three theories have resulted. This monster is the fruit of Celtic traditions and would be identical to the Cath Paluc of the medieval Welsh *Llyfr Du Caerfyrddin* (Black Book of Carmarthen), which exists in a manuscript copied between 1154 and 1189.[10] Here, too, the monster comes from the waters, this time those of the sea, and lays waste to the land, but he is slain by Arthur's seneschal, Kay. Another interpretation sees *palu* as a form of Latin *palus,* meaning "swamp." The cat would thereby be a marsh spirit or swamp demon. We know from the *Vita Godehardi episcopi prior* (Life of Bishop Godehard), written by Wolfher of Hildesheim around 1054, that swamps were filled with terrifying glamors and illusions. Wolfher mentions a "horrible marsh" near Hildesheim "where ghastly illusions (*horribiles illusiones*) could be seen and heard day and night."[11] In the clerical lexicon, "illusion" meant "apparition." The final theory, recently put forth by Philippe Walter, suggests that behind *palu* is the term *pelu,* meaning "hairy." Chapalu would therefore take us back to the major figure of the wild man who, depending on the location, could also assume animal shapes.[12] This is an interesting view of things because the wild man can be regarded as the carnival-like form of a spirit from an earlier time, and he is also a manifestation of the chaotic, natural forces that continually threaten human society.

In his *History of the Danes,* Saxo Grammaticus includes two passages that concern the history of local land spirits, although they are concealed behind the embellishments of literary fantasy. Having squandered his father's treasury on war, Frothi is seeking more funds. One of the locals tells him: "Now here, rising in slopes, lies an island whose hills conceal a rich hoard of treasure. The guardian of the mount keeps the choice pile, a dragon intricately twined and curled in multiple spirals, dragging the sinuous folds of its tail, lashing its manifold coils and vomiting poison." Frothi goes to the island alone, "with no more company to attack the monster than when champions fight a duel" (which brings King Arthur to mind), slays the monster, and takes possession of the local riches (II, 38). The dragon is one of a thousand forms adopted by land spirits, and analogous tales have heroes and dwarves as their protagonists. In another passage, Saxo tells us of *virgines silvestres,* "forest maidens" (III, 70). Led astray by an unusual mist while hunting, Høther comes to the home of the forest maidens. They predict his future, then the house and its occupants vanish and Høther finds himself under the open sky. It has long been acknowledged that these maidens are the Norns, the Germanic Parcae, but their presence in the forest shows that wild places are, in some way, an antechamber of the Other World, which explains their value as a haven for all kinds of spirits and genies.

An attentive reader of medieval texts will notice other traces of land spirits. The *Gesta Herwardi* (Deeds of Hereward the Wake), which dates from the middle of the twelfth century, mentions a crowd that asks questions of a well at night. The *Miracula S. Mathiae* (Miracles of Saint Matthew), also written in the twelfth century, speaks of a child that fell from a skiff into the Moselle river. "A young man stripped off his clothes and dove into the water seeking to rescue the child, but an evil spirit, which they called Neptune, held him back" (*maligno spiritu retrahente, quem Neptuno vocant*).[13] As we have seen, "Neptune" is the scholarly name the clerics used to designate water spirits, but there are other names and Gervase of Tilbury uses *dracus:*

> As for dracs . . . , it is said they live in the depths of rivers and by taking on the appearance of gold rings or cups floating on the water, they attract women and children bathing by the riversides; indeed when such people attempt to catch the objects they have seen, they are abruptly grabbed and dragged down into the watery depths. (*Otia Imperialia,* III, 85)

In the *Helgisaga Óláfs konungs Haraldssonar,* which is known as the *Oldest Saga of Saint Olaf* or the *Legendary Saga of Saint Olaf,* King Olaf is seeking shelter for the night in the mountains and asks Busi if he knows of one (chap. 67). The other replies: "Certainly, Sire, it is called Gröningar, but no one should stay there as it is haunted by trolls and evil spirits" (*fyrir trollagange oc meinvætta*).

We may now summarize what we have observed. In the hagiographies, the most common form taken by land spirits is the dragon, but the narrative literature has added to this giants, dwarves, fairies, and so on, as we will discover. In every case the identity of the spirits is evident through a recurring theme, which is that of desertification, the waste land. But behind this there may also be theme of human sacrifices demanded by a beast living close to a human community: it will only

Local spirits sometimes became dwarves encountered by the hero in the wild.
Illustration from the Heldenbuch *(Book of Heroes).*
Strassburg: Johann Prüss, ca. 1483.

leave them alone on the condition that they regularly give it offerings of individual persons or animals. While the symbolism of Christianity's war against paganism is particularly overt here—so much so that the ancient substrata is practically obliterated—it is still possible to discern traces of rites intended to tame or neutralize local forces from before the area was settled by humans. It is also worth noting that the saints only tame the monsters, leaving it up to the local inhabitants to slay them.

Moreover, all these legends reveal that local land spirits are only driven away by a sacred force that is superior to the powers they have at their disposal. In the romances and in the less Christianized Norse texts, rites persist in which the heroes act as civilizing figures who expand the boundaries of cultivated land and cause the virgin, wild spaces to recede. These wild spaces are truly the last refuge of the spirits. Comparison between the sources allows us to detect the various strata that make up those texts with their combinations of extremely archaic elements, folk beliefs, and Christianity. This brings us to the notion of boundaries and frontiers.

12

Taking Possession of a Piece of Land

It is in the Germanic-Scandinavian countries that the rites accompanying the taking possession of a piece of land are most clear. In other countries, the data from historiography and hagiography is harder to interpret and resists decipherment until the point at which one has some material available for crosschecking and comparison. I am going to start, therefore, with examples from the Icelandic *Book of Settlements*.

Initially, the colonists who travelled to Iceland entrusted the god they worshipped with the task of indicating the site of their future settlement. As they neared the shore, they threw the posts of the high-seat, which they had brought with them from their former home, overboard. The high-seat was the seat of honor reserved for the use of the master of the house, and it was often carved with the image of a god. As an example, we may take a look at what Ingolf did. He began by consulting the auguries after having performed a sacrifice and learned that he needed to move to Iceland. He fitted out his ship and set sail. "When he spied land, he threw the posts of his high-seat into the water 'for luck' (*til heilla*) and said that he would live wherever they came ashore. He claimed the land at this spot, which was now called Ingólfshöfði" (S 8).

The sacred value of this action is clearly explained by a passage from the *Vatnsdæla Saga* (Saga of the People of the Lake Valley). The god Freyr stole Ingimund's amulet and hid it in Iceland. A seer came to Ingimund and told him he would find it by digging the ground where, after disembarking, he had set the posts of his high-seat (chap. 10–15). It was therefore up to the gods, at least in certain cases, to determine the site on which their protégés would settle.

When Thórolf Mostrarskegg, a worshipper of Thor, came within sight of Iceland, he threw the posts of his high-seat overboard. "Thor was carved on it. He declared that Thor would land where he wanted him to dwell, and he made a vow to consecrate to Thor all the land he colonized and to name it after him" (S 85). The cape where the posts floated ashore is called Thórsnes, "Thor's Cape," and Thórolf settled nearby.

Despite the terse nature of the sagas, the role played by the columns of the high-seat is decisive. Here are two examples from the *Laxdæla Saga* (Saga of the People of the Salmon Valley). Unn found the pillars of her high-seat at the head of Breiðafjörðr. "She felt it was perfectly clear where she should take up residence; she had a farm built at the site, now called Hvamm, and lived there" (chap. 5). Bjorn and his people behaved in the same way: "It appeared to them that they [the high-seat posts] indicated the place they should settle" (chap. 3).

Beyond any particular religion, human beings think in similar ways, and I feel I should point out an interesting parallel that shows the true extent to which Christianity is tributary of ancestral, pagan tradition. A passage from the *Book of Settlements* clearly forms a junction between the pagan and the Christian world.

When Örlygg left for Iceland, Bishop Patrek asked him to carry lumber with which to make a church, an iron bell, and a plenarium (a liturgical book containing a missal, breviary, and periscopes), as well as "the consecrated soil to be placed beneath the corner columns. The bishop then asked him to claim the land where he saw two mountains coming out of the sea," and Patrek gave an exact description of the place where Örlygg should settle (S 15). This passage copies the pagan rites precisely: no high-seat posts but consecrated earth, which is to say it bears the same religious value of the posts sculpted in Thor's likeness. Furthermore, Patrek behaves exactly like a seeress (*spákona*) or like the three Finns (Sámi) who are sent to retrieve Ingimund's amulet.

In many lives of the saints we find a theme that is quite close to what we have just seen: a churchman entrusts God with the task of choosing the place for his establishment and this takes place as follows. The *Vita S. Carantoci* (Life of Saint Carantoc), written around 1100, tells how Carantoc, who had come from Kerediciaun (Cardigan), reached the mouth of the Severn after having "entrusted his altar to the waves" (*misit altare in mare*) in order to learn, in accordance to the place where it landed, on what side of the river "God wishes him to direct his steps" (*ubi Deus volebat illum venire*). When he found his altar, he built a church on that spot.[1]

These legends come in another form that is suggestive of the same mentality. The relics of Saint Vincent, abandoned on a boat, are supposed to have come ashore near Lisbon, and since that time the saint's ship has figured in the city's coat of arms. On other occasions, as in the case of the Boulogne-sur-Mer's Virgin of the Boat, it was a statuette that

Boulogne-sur-Mer's Virgin of the Boat

arrived on a skiff, and a sanctuary was built to house it. The decapitated body of Saint Tropez reached shore carried by a marvelous ship. And in some cases, no doubt is left as to the topical character of the "deity." In the legend of Saint Christine of Viserny, for example, the chapel built for her was found completely destroyed the following morning. After a vexing period, the irate workers cast down their tools yelling: "If this place is not suitable, fine! May our hammers and trowels be carried to the desired spot." The tools were found the next day atop the mountain, and the chapel was built there without difficulty.[2]

It is also necessary to reexamine all those stories in which decapitated saints carry their heads to the spot where they wish to be buried. In these cephalophoric legends, the result is always the same: a sanctuary is quickly built and miracles are created by the presence of the holy body.[3] In other words, a new space has been sanctified and the body (or relics and so forth) of the dead individual is the visible form of a tutelary function. In nearly every case the saint first transforms into a tutelary spirit, and then sometimes into a land spirit, but the two aspects are originally distinct as it involves opposing one form of the sacred to another, and ensuring protection against the powers haunting the site. This is even more blatant when a pilgrimage becomes established that brings prosperity to the monastery or village in which the holy tomb is located.[4]

We can compare these kinds of stories with those in which astounding events designate the site of a future human settlement. It is by following a more or less wondrous animal that the colonizer discovers a place that suits him, or it may even be a flight of birds that confers a particular value to a site. On the Portuguese side of the Algarves, the place called *Promontorium sacrum* carries the name "Port of the Raven Gods," and it was already considered sacred in the Roman era. According to the Pseudo-Plutarch, the choice of the site where the town of Lugdunum was built was determined by a flight of ravens in 43 BCE. It so happens that the Celts believed that the raven was the sacred bird of the god Lugh. Plancus, the colonizer, used his plow to trace the two primary roads of the colony with his head ritually covered by his toga.[5]

In his *Topography of Ireland,* Gerald of Wales reported the following:

> Also in Italy, near the noble city of Ravenna, all kinds of ravens, crows, and blackbirds coming from all regions of Italy gather every year on the day of Saint Apollinaire, as if they had arranged a rendezvous. Thanks to ancient custom, they are given the corpse of a horse on this day. If you were to ask me the reason for this, I could scarcely explain it, except as it is perhaps a custom started so long ago that it has become almost natural. There where the body of the saint was laid, the birds gather, or rather, they are brought together by a miracle of this saint. It is from this gathering that comes the belief that Ravenna was first called Ravennesburch, which in the German tongue means "City of the Ravens.[6]

Here we can clearly see the superimposition of pagan and Christian elements: the ancient phenomenon is tied to the anniversary feast of a saint, so there is the annual renewal of a highly religious propitiatory rite inasmuch as it is a horse that is sacrificed (the importance of horses in the religion of the ancient Germans is well known). The offering was most likely addressed to the guardian spirits of the place.

In the legend of Saint Michael, it is the unusual behavior of a bull that allows a sacred site to be discovered:

> In the Year of our Lord 390, there was a man in the town of Siponto who, according to several authors, was named Garganus from the name of this mountain, or else the mountain was named after this man. He owned an immense flock of sheep and immense herd of cattle. One day as these animals were grazing over the mountainsides, one bull left the others to climb to the summit and did not return with the herd.
>
> His owner took a large number of his servants in search of him and they finally found him on the mountaintop by the entrance to a cave. Irritated that this bull had ventured off on his own, the man

immediately shot a poisoned arrow at him but in an instant, as if pushed by the wind, the arrow came back and struck the person who shot it.

The terrified inhabitants sought out the bishop and asked for his counsel regarding such a strange occurrence. He ordered three days of fasting and told them they should ask an explanation of God. After which, Saint Michael appeared to the bishop and told him, "You know that this man was struck by his own dart by my will for I am the Archangel Michael who, with the intention of dwelling in this spot on earth and keeping it safe, had wished it be known through this sign that I am the chief and guardian of this place."[7]

Of course, Saint Michael soon had his sanctuary. This text by Jacobus de Voragine is abounding with pagan elements and Philippe Walter, some time ago, revealed three of them: the discovery of a sacred site by an animal; the arrow that turns back on the one who looses it; and the name Garganus carried by of the cowherd of the mountain of Saint Michael.[8] We could add the declaration by Michael, which is that of a veritable genius loci. Saint Michael appeared again around the year 710 in Tumba (Mount Tombe, which today is called Tomberlaine),* near the sea not far from Avranches, and commanded the bishop there to build a church at that spot in celebration of his memory, like the one on Monte Gargano. The archangel stated that it should be erected there where "they find a bull that thieves had hidden." This is what happened and after various events, this mountain of Saint Michael was Christianized.

In the legend of Notre-Dame-de-Bon-Encontre, near Agen, it is again a bull that allows the right place to be discovered:

In Pau, a hamlet of Sainte-Radegonde parish, lived the Fraissinet brothers who owned a field and a barn in La Roqual. The youngest

---

*In Tombe-Elaine, the second term is, in fact, a distortion of the divine name Belenos. This place was sacred for the Gauls, perhaps because it was regularly struck by lightning.

brother had seen one of his oxen leave the herd on several occasions to throw itself down on the ground next to a bush. Intrigued, he ran toward the ox and, in the densely growing thorny bushes, spied a small image of the Virgin holding her Son in her arms. He brought it back to his mother who locked it in a chest so as to show it later to the family. But when she opened the chest, the statuette had vanished and the next day, thanks to the ox's behavior, it was found again in the bushes. This kept happening and eventually a chapel was built on the spot where it had been found, and the statue was placed within it.[9]

This legend, reported in 1642 by Vincent, a Franciscan, testifies to the persistence of ancient ways of thinking and shows how it was believed that "gods" were firmly connected to places. In Faubouloin (Morvan), an ox that regularly escaped from the herd led the cowherd to an ash near a spring, where a statue of the Madonna was discovered, and a chapel was then erected on this site. The animal guide is common to many cities. In Bern (Alemannic Switzerland) a she-bear (*Bärin*) guided the city's founder, Berthold V, Duke of Zähringen, to a site where the goddess Artio was worshipped (as an inscription on an ancient bronze statue found there informs us). As we have seen, spirits often take on the appearance of an animal to guide humans to a site.

The gods are not the only ones who can decide where humans can settle; the dead can do so as well. Before dying on the boat carrying him to Iceland, Kveldulf (whose name means "Evening Wolf") asked that his coffin be tossed into the sea and for his son to build his house a short distance from the place where his body came ashore.[10] As we saw earlier, the dead become a conduit between men and the supernatural powers. Continuing to live in their graves, they can help the living and foil the plots of their enemies. It is not rare to come across remarks like the following in the *Laxdæla Saga:* "I wish to be buried in Skáneyjarfjall," said Odd as he died, "from there I can see the entire region."[11] The underlying meaning is that "there I will be able to keep an eye on my family's doings."

Once the home site has been chosen, it is time for the rite of taking possession of the soil, and there are several rituals for this purpose.[12] We may look at the example of Ævarr. He goes back up the Blandá, and when he reaches the place called Mobergsbrekkur, he sticks a large staff into the ground and declares that this is where his son Véfröd will build his house.[13] This is a common action and can be seen in the place-names. Thórolf Mostrarskegg claims the land between the Stafá (River of the Staff) and the Thórsá (Thor's River). Rodrek, Hrosskell's slave, takes possession of the land by "sticking in the ground his staff that has been freshly stripped of bark," which is called *landkönnud,* meaning "settlement mark" (S 194). One might also be satisfied, like Náttfari, to make marks on the trees (S 247), but since this individual is later expelled from his lands, we can deduce that this approach is not truly according to ritual. As Jacob Grimm points out elsewhere, however, the marking of trees sets the boundaries for a sacred space.[14] It is possible that the use of wood refers to tree worship.

Sæmund follows another rite. He takes possession of his lands by "carrying fire around his land-claim" (S 189). This mysterious turn of phrase is illuminated thanks to another passage from the *Book of Settlements:* "Önund shot a flaming arrow over the river and thereby consecrated the land to the west and lived between the rivers" (S 198). The *Víga-Glúms saga* says the same thing (chap. 26). Helgi the Lean colonized all the Eyjafjord between Sigluness and Reynisness, and made a large fire at the spot where the lake spilled into the sea every year, "thereby consecrating the entire fjord between the capes" (H 184).

Fire allegedly drives away land spirits because it is connected to the sun, which is the enemy of chthonic creatures. It petrifies dwarves, for example, and is the absolute master of natural forces. Two common sayings express this fact: *fara með eldi at fornum sið ok nema sér land* (to go with fire according to the ancient custom and take the land), and *fara (um) land eldi* (walk the circumference of the land with fire). King Harald Fairhair may have been the one who codified the rites called *eldvigning,* "consecration by fire," but they preexisted him. The *Book of Settlements* (H 294) states:

> The king stipulated that none should take land that he could not travel across in one day with fire and his equipage. The fire had to be kindled when the sun was in the east; it was necessary to build fires from place to place so that the last could be seen from the next, and the fires that were made when the sun was in the east had to burn until nightfall. Next they had to walk to where the sun hung in the west and make more fires.

The act of taking possession of land therefore took from sunrise to sunset. In this regard, Régis Boyer notes that the worship of fire in the northern regions was paralleled by a worship of light, which dispersed spirits of all kinds. This point is made strikingly clear in the *Guta saga* (Saga of the Gotlanders):

> Gotland was first discovered by a man named Thjelvar. At this time, Gotland was an enchanted island (*elvist,* "elfen") that sank during the day beneath the waves and surfaced at night. This man was the first one to bring fire to the island and it has not sunk since that time.[15]

Jean-Marie Maillefer remarks that "it is tempting to compare the name of Gotland's first colonist, Thjelvar, which is rare and only attested in Swedish anthroponymy by a runic inscription of Östergötland (Ostrogothia), with the name Thjalvi, servant of the god Thor, whose characteristic natural element is fire and whose traditional role is to fight against the forces that are foreign to the human world." In the *Saga of Víga-Glúm* (chap. 26), Einar's mother goes to Thvera with fire, compels Glúm to leave the place, and states that she has sanctified the land for her son (*er helgat landit Einari syni minum*).

There are simpler ways to appropriate the land than the one just described. In numerous charters, the most important passages of which Jacob Grimm collected in his *Deutsche Rechtsalterthümer* (German Legal Antiquities), taking possession of land could also be achieved by throwing a hammer, which, as we know, is the attribute of the god Thor. This was the case in 1360 in the archbishopric of Mainz.[16] On the boundaries defined this way, the sign of the hammer would be carved according to the *Saga of Haakon the Good* (chap. 18). An axe can also be used when it involves setting the boundary of a forest or a body of water, a rite attested in 1121 and 1306. Many centuries earlier, the legal code of the Bavarii, *Lex Baiuwariorum,* mentioned a great axe in the following rite. If a farm is not enclosed (*cinctus*), someone contesting the boundary shall toss a great axe at noon toward the east and toward the west. It is forbidden to do this toward the north: no hedge can be placed there; the shadow will mark the border (XI, 6, 2).[17]

I will remind the reader in passing that in the legend of Romulus, possession of the land was established by a spear toss on the Palatine Hill. In the legend of Saint Gonçalo of Amarante, the choice of the building site was chosen by the play of the saint's staff, and in a rite of *Terminatio* perpetuated in Catalonia by Miguel de Iranzo in 1407, the setting of the boundaries (*limites*) was decided by casting a spear. Casting spears or hammers is a means of intimidating the spirits, equivalent to a declaration of war—or at the very least it is a manifestation of the will of the colonist who, strengthened by his own gods or by his own "luck," as the ancient Scandinavians termed it, has no doubts about achieving his ends.

A flaming arrow (Old Icelandic *tindrör*) could be shot over coveted territory. It was also possible to combine several means of taking possession. The *Book of Settlements* describes a group of these that has no equivalent elsewhere in the text:

> Einar and his two brothers, Vestmad and Vémund, buried an axe in the Reistargnúp, which was consequently renamed Ax Fjord. They placed an eagle on high in the West and called this spot Eagle's Tuft;

at a third spot they placed a cross, and called this place Cross Ridge.
In this way they consecrated the entire Ax Fjord.

Other passages in the *Book of Settlements* emphasize the duration
of the operation: it takes two to three days. It seems that this difference
is explained by the then existing legislation that decreed a difference
between men and women. According to the directives of King Harald
Fairhair, a woman marked off the boundaries of her future domain by
leading a two-year old heifer, which implies a slow pace. It so happens
that in the *Book of Settlements,* one passage implies the land can be circumscribed by riding a mare. Vébjörn marks off his plot from Horse
Fjord to a piece of land called Folafótr ("Foal's Foot"),[18] which would
confirm the legend of Saint Andreas (discussed below).

It should be apparent to the reader that Christian thought and
pagan thought function in the same manner. The colonizers placed
themselves under the protection of a god—Thor, for example, or the
Christian God—but in every case, there are two sacred forces that
opposed each other: the original sacred power, represented by the land
spirits, and the sacred power of the colonist. It cannot be doubted that
all these acts involved the application of a sacred ritual, as the recur-
rence of the verb "to consecrate" (*heilla*) clearly indicates. The individual is therefore seeking in fact to substitute one sacred power (for
example, that of the god who guides the colonist's steps) for another
(that of the unsettled lands ruled by their masters, the land spirit masters). The rite of possessing a piece of land seeks to drive the spirits outside the marked off space. The *landvættir* are thereby obliged to tolerate
the colonist's presence on their lands; their power has been dispelled
but, as we shall see, that does not mean they have vanished. They even
retain some power as they can bring prosperity and become household
spirits, but they regain all their destructive capabilities if the rites are no
longer respected.

13

Circumambulation

Appropriation, Expropriation, and Protection Rites

From what we have seen, it is clear that taking possession of a piece of land often included a circumambulation, which is first and foremost a circumscription. In other words, this means that the notion of the circle, whether a perfect one or not, is of the highest importance.

The rites of circumambulation need to be read on two levels. They involve the protection of the circumscribed space against external forces—the land spirits whose ownership of the land predates that of the human settler—and also confirm the unique sacredness of a piece of land. This sacredness can be based on the presence of a god or, as was the case for Christians, the presence of a saint or a holy relic. It can also be based on the presence of a tamed spirit or that of a dead individual— often the first colonist, who has returned as a guardian spirit. The circumambulation is one of the oldest forms of establishing ownership of a piece of land and has a value equivalent to that of a legal writ. We keep in mind, however, that in this older period law and religion were inseparable.

Some of the oldest evidence we have concerns the history of the founding of Rome. Romulus and Remus followed the omens, in this case the flight of the vultures. Then, when they decided upon the Palatine Hill, which was held by Romulus, he drew the outer boundaries of the future city with a plow harnessed to two oxen. We know what happened next. Remus scoffed at this enclosure, an easily crossed ditch, leapt over it, and Romulus slew him for this sacrilege. In fact, this ancient Italic rite was a consecration ritual. According to other traditions, the plow had to be pulled by a white bull and a white cow. Titus Livy (II, 5) tells us that Horatius Cocles was given ownership of the fields that he surrounded with a furrow in one day (*uno die circumararit*). It so happens that this furrow, the *mundus,* formed the meeting point between the lower realms and the earthly world, as Mircea Eliade saw so clearly. "When the *mundus* is open it is as if the gates of the gloomy infernal gods were open," says Varro (cited by Macrobius, *Saturnalia* I, 16, 18).[1]

François Delpech notes that during the nineteenth century in Catalonia a similar rite existed to the one used in the founding of Rome. The text on which he bases his claim states:

> In Gelida, until the last half of the last century, when it was necessary to build a house, the perimeter it required was marked out by a furrow drawn by a plow. The furrow was not one continuous line; the plow would be lifted up at the places where the doors would go. It was believed that if this was not done, the house would collapse.[2]

Catalan traditions also say that the town of Villareal was founded by King James I of Aragon, "who personally used a plow to mark out the contours of the city and its streets with furrows." There is another rite from this same province that is worth noting:

> In Cardadeu, there was a family whose heir, on the afternoon of Carnival Sunday, plowed the square to indicate his ancient claim of ownership over the village.

This is no less than a renewal of a rite for taking ownership of a land.

Furthermore, every sacred building was laid out according to a specific rite. A team of oxen opened furrows at the four points of a square starting at the southern side and working their way around it in a carefully defined order and direction. Moreover, the priests who read the auspices and auguries, after having divided up the celestial region (*regions caeli*) with the help of a curved staff, "freed and declared empty" the future building site. "What is then inaugurated is put in communication, in an effective symmetry, with the heavens . . . ; what is not inaugurated remains essentially earthbound," notes Georges Dumézil.[3] "The Italic temple," says Eliade, "was the zone where the upper (divine), terrestrial, and subterranean worlds intersected."[4]

Snorri Sturluson twice tells the story of Gefjon who, in mythological times, took possession of the land that today forms the Danish island of Seeland:

> As reward for the entertainment she had given him, Gylfi, king of Sweden, granted a woman named Gefjon "as much farm land in his kingdom that four oxen can plow in one day and night. . . . She went to Jötunheimr [Giant-land] in the north for four oxen—which were her own sons conceived with a giant—and yoked them to a plow. They went forward so powerfully and dug so deeply, that an entire piece of land became detached. The oxen dragged it west toward the sea. . . . There Gefjon anchored the land and gave it a name: she called it Seeland. (*Gylfaginning*, chap. 1)[5]

In the *Saga of the Ynglings,* Snorri indicates that Odin sent Gefjon in search of new lands. "She came to King Gylfi, and he gave her a ploughland. Then she went to Giant-land and there bore four sons to some giant. She transformed them into oxen and attached them to the plough and drew the land westward into the sea, opposite Óðin's Island [Odense], and that is [now] called Selund [Seeland], and that is where she dwelled afterwards."[6]

Many texts that are of a strictly legal nature describe the appropriation of land by similar actions.

In 496, Clovis granted to Jean, the abbot of Reomans (Burgundy), as much land as he could traverse while perched on his ass during the time of siesta (midday). Flodoard tells the same story about Saint Remy (*Historia Remensis ecclesiae*, I, 14). Jakob Twinger's *Chronicle* of Konigshöfen (Alsace) says that Dagobert gifted Saint Florent, or Florentin, with the land he crossed while riding a she-ass, during the time it took him to get out of his bath and get dressed.

In the *Life of Saint Malo,* written at the end of the eleventh century by the deacon Beli, Malo commanded Domnech:

> In the name of Christ, son of God, take two young, untrained oxen and place them in a single yoke, followed by a plow, and I will give you all the land they can walk around between sunrise and sunset (*de ortu solis ad occasum*) as your personal property, for eternal life, and in perpetual ownership, and may whoever changes anything, despite you and your authority, be cursed by your prayer.[7]

The end of this passage strongly resembles a curse spell.

Around 1205, Waldemar, king of Denmark, gave Saint Andreas, in Slagelse, as much land as he could mark off while riding a nine-day-old mare while he [the king] bathed. The chapel in Kervédot, in the French commune of Quimper, has a wooden statue depicting Saint Théleau traveling through his parish mounted on a stag. Louis the Pious granted Henri the Guelph the land he could mark off with a plow during the time he slept at midday. During the expansion of Zittau in 1255 by Ottokar II of Bohemia, a furrow was drawn while the king and high nobility of the kingdom followed on horseback. Charlemagne's capitulary *De villis* (§27) says that the land belongs to whoever can circumnavigate it in a single day (*in unum die circumire*). Meanwhile the *Indiculus superstitionum* (§23) condemns the rite of drawing furrows around dwellings, which is a protective measure. We should recall that even in the nineteenth century a rite like this was still practiced in Catalonia when a house was built.

We can probably compare this measure to another rite denounced by Caesarius of Arles. This rite involved walking around houses disguised as a stag, cow, or some other portentous animal. The Arles council banned it in 578. Unfortunately, the texts do not tell us the purpose of these actions, but more recent examples, collected by ethnologists in Central Europe in the 1950s, suggest that wearing this disguise refers to some minor deity.

Such rites are basically similar to the following one, which takes place on a parallel plane: this is the renovation of the sacred status of a property, its "refounding." In the middle of the fourteenth century, a resident of Luneburg ran around his farm holding his chimney hook in the direction of the sun's course to protect it against the plague. He then buried the hook beneath the doorsill. A certain Rand was said to have paraded a likeness of Thor around his island for protection,[8] a rite that should probably be compared to the entry from the *Indiculus superstitionium* that forbade the carrying of an idol through the fields (*De simulacro quod per campos portant*).

When an epidemic broke out in Soissons circa 1135–1140, the relics of Saint Gregory were paraded around the ramparts. This meant that the city was being surrounded by an impenetrable and invisible spiritual barrier, thus establishing a sacred space, inside of which the saint's action would be made more effective. A similar procedure was described earlier by Gregory of Tours (*De Gloria Confessorum,* chap. 78) and can be seen again in eleventh-century Flanders where a circumambulation was organized around the Lobbes Abbey. In the twelfth century, the head of Saint Calentine was paraded around Jumièges monastery to drive the rats away, according to Baudri de Bourgueil. Once we recognize that illnesses were believed to be sent by spirits, malcontent genies, or demons, it is easy to see the pagan backdrop of these measures.

Processions of lights that are led over the places requiring exorcism have formed part of the liturgical practice of Christians since the fourth century, but they have earlier parallels in the Roman Ambarvalia and the rite of Amburbium. I would also point out that the Rogations (from Latin *rogare,* "to ask") were instituted in Brioude by Saint Gallus during the epidemic of 543–546, following the example set by Saint Mamertus, bishop of Vienne (in the Dauphiné region), in 470. Jacobus de Voragine recounts the following in *The Golden Legend:*

> Vienne was afflicted by frequent and frightening earthquakes that knocked down many houses and churches. During the night repeated noises and clamoring could be heard. . . . Just as, through God's permission, the demons once entered the swine, they similarly through God's permission, for the sins of men, entered wolves. . . . As these misfortunes were happening daily, the holy bishop Mamertus commanded a three-day fast and instituted litanies.

Jacobus de Voragine also recalls that the principal rite of this celebration was "a procession in which the cross and the banner were carried; the bells were also rung so that the demons would be terrified and flee."[9]

Elsewhere, the circumambulation is given concrete representation by chains. In Thuringia and Bavaria, the chapels of Saint Leonard are located on hills and in forests that are surrounded this way. It so happens that sanctuaries and sacred spaces of the ancient Germans were surrounded by a string, which can also be glimpsed in the legend of the founding of Carthage (this will be examined in depth later) and clearly appears in the thirteenth-century Middle High German poem *Laurin.* In the heart of the Tyrolean mountains, the king of the dwarves who bears this name owns a marvelous rose garden whose fence is a silk thread (69–72). Whoever breaks this thread will be subject to his vengeance.

We should note that the Bible clearly indicates how the sacred nature of a place can be nullified in a certain way. This means its defenses have been lessened because a new circumambulation has been performed. Jehovah told Joshua:

And ye shall compass the city, all ye men of war, and go round about the city once. Thus shalt thou do six days. And seven priests shall bear before the ark seven trumpets of rams' horns: and the seventh day ye shall compass the city seven times, and the priests shall blow the trumpets. And it shall come to pass, that when they make a long blast with the ram's horn, and when ye hear the sound of the trumpet, all the people shall shout with a great shout; and the wall of the city shall fall down flat. (Joshua 6:3–5, KJV)

This complex operation that implements a variety of measures is a reversal of the circumambulation as a means of defense. The sacred power of the Israelites, their God if you will, whose help is represented by the ark and the ram's horn, is stronger than the city's guardian spirits.

In 1590, in North Berwick (England) an assembly of witches took place. They walked around the church in the opposite direction of the sun (*wittershins*) and then one of the witches blew on the keyhole, the locks opened, the profane coven entered, and the devil revealed himself in the pulpit to his followers in the form of a black man. The operation clearly indicates that the supernatural protection the church enjoyed had been nullified, which permitted this sabbath to take place in a consecrated building.[10] Moreover, in a great many rites of witchcraft, there is a reversed circumambulation, which is indicated here by *wittershins,* a valuable piece of information that was provided earlier by medieval sagas in which the term is *andsoelis.* This reversal gives free rein to spirits of all kinds, liberating the forces of chaos and therefore the land spirits who have been contained or conciliated by the appropriate rites. But this does not seem to have always been the case.

In the Hænsna-Þóris saga (Saga of Hen-Thorir), which describes actions taking place in Iceland between 930 and 999, an interesting passage stands out that is worthy of attention:

Thorir burned Blundketil in his farm of Örnolfsdalr. A short time later, Odd arrived on the scene. He went to a certain house that was not entirely burned and there took hold of a birch rafter and, with a tug, pulled it from the building. The brand then burst back into flame and he rode widdershins around the whole farm saying, "I hereby take ownership for I see no trace of inhabited property. Let all those who hear me be witnesses."[11]

There is good reason to ask why Odd rode in the direction opposite the course of the sun, and this necessitates an explanation that, alas, can be no more than a hypothesis. It seems as if two different rites are superimposed here: one is the well-known rite of taking possession by fire; the other (his declaration) is magical and accompanies a circumambulation, no doubt intended to drive the spirits of the dead away from this place and protect oneself from their vengeance, which is ever a possibility. But there is also another conceivable explanation: an abandoned spot will be immediately reoccupied by the land spirits that the first inhabitant had chased off. Whatever the actual reason, the fire plus the widdershins circumambulation clearly indicates that Odd feared something, and the sole purpose of his action was to show witnesses that he was taking possession of an estate.

The sacred nature of a site can also be restored through a circumambulation. In Snorri's recounting of *Saint Óláf's Saga*, King Olaf's men have trampled a field and spoiled the harvest. The peasant comes to Olaf to complain and the king decides to right this wrong: "the king rode up to the field and saw that the whole field had been flattened. He *rode around it* and then said, 'I do expect, my man, that God will repair the damage done you, and I believe this field of yours will be restored in a week's time.' And indeed the field recovered excellently, as the king had said."[12] Only the detail I italicized makes it possible to see that a rite of sanctification had been performed. According to Gregory of Tours (*History of the Franks*, IV, 14), the first task of the new king was to make the tour around his kingdom on horseback, which is a measure for taking possession.

The persistence of certain practices is quite astonishing and in the

Acta S. Goeznovici (*Acts of the Life of Saint Gouesnou*), which dates from 1019, they seem to practically leap off the pages. Count Comorre granted Gouesnou as much land for his monastery as he could enclose with ditches in a single day. He agreed to a day and a time, before which the holy man would have had to finish his circuit (*assignata est dies qua sanctus debuit terram circuire*). Our man then headed north, with a pitchfork dragging on the ground behind him—"and as he dragged this rude fork, a strange thing happened, the dirt rose up on either side and formed a large ditch." He walked for a stade, then turned east and went straight ahead to a place called "Caput nemoris," which is today Penhoat ("Wooden Head"). From there he turned right and headed south, and having walked in a straight line for around four stades, then turned westward and walked another four stades toward the north, whereupon he finally turned east to return to his starting point.[13] It so happens that this method is the exact counterpart to the way the sacred square is drawn by the Romans and Indo-Europeans (see diagram below), as Georges Dumézil showed in his study of the demarcation of the *āhavanīya,* the fire over which offerings are passed on to the gods.[14]

There are rites for claiming ownership of a plot of ground, even though they may seem more like figments of legend, which at one time or another corresponded with existing realities before they lost their sacred character and were devalued more or less to the status of simple motifs for fables. Such is the case for the legend of Carthage's founding by Dido.[15] A bull hide cut into thin strips was used to mark off the ter-

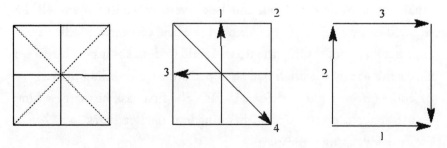

Drawing of the sacred square after Georges Dumézil

ritory of the city; in other words, to form an enclosed space (whether round or square does not matter). The same method was used to establish the boundaries of the future city of London (if we can believe the *Saga of Ragnar Loðbrók*), and even those of York. There is also the case of the Melusine legend, as told by Jean d'Arras at the end of the fourteenth century. The fairy advises Raymondin of Poitiers:

> Ask of young Count Bertrand . . . as much land as you can enclose within a deer hide. He should give you full franchise to this land. . . . On the next day, you shall meet a man carrying a sack of deer hides tanned in alum. Buy them from him . . . then have them cut into a single strip that is as thin as it can possibly be. Next, go back to your place, where you shall find the boundaries all drawn and prepared in accordance with my plans and desires. And at the moment you prepare to join the two ends of the strip, if the strip grows, take it down into the valley, and know that the water of the spring there, by flowing through it, shall form a small river that will be of great use in this place.

Thanks to this strategy, Raymondin becomes the owner of a vast land, whose site was selected by the fairy—she is the counterpart of the gods or dead ancestors in the texts cited above—and she provided the means of appropriating it. At the predicted time, Raymondin encountered two strangers:

> They made a skein of the leather strip and carried it into the valley, as close as possible to the rock cliff. They planted a solid stake to which they attached one end of the strip. . . . They then completed a circuit around the whole mountain and when they returned to their starting point, they found a long length of leather was left over, which they pulled down along the length of the valley. . . . A stream gushed out at this spot.[16]

Coudrette, who independently of Jean d'Arras tells the same story, says:

> It was then two strangers appeared who took the deerskin lace and wound it into an enormous ball. They buried a stake in the ground at one spot and attached the lace to it, then surrounded, including the mountain and spring described above, a vast expanse of the plain below as far as the stream that flowed there.[17]

Count Bertrand's reaction is eloquent. "This is indeed quite strange. It looks like fairy work to me."

Let's now summarize the information we have gleaned from these various accounts. The choice of where humans should settle is entrusted to supernatural beings, to God, or to gods, or in liaison with them (saints, the dead, fairies). Behind the various rites—demarcation by fire, furrow, a strip, or by riding—there is an essential element of the operation that stands out: the creation of an enclosed space, a cultivated space in all the meanings of the word, which will stand in opposition to the savagery of untamed nature, which is always associated with primordial chaos. As noted by Mircea Eliade, these chaotic expanses "still participate in the undifferentiated, formless modality of pre-Creation. This is why, when possession is taken of a territory—that is, when its exploitation begins—rites are performed that symbolically repeat the act of Creation: the uncultivated area is first 'cosmicized,' then inhabited."[18] Through the rituals of taking possession of land, chaos is transformed into cosmos through imitating the gods.

This transformation takes place by the "neutralization" of natural forces, manifestations of original chaos represented by the local land spirits. Before examining this more extensively, we will take a closer look at the notion of enclosure and the marking of boundaries.

14

Boundaries and Their Markers

The study of the boundaries of colonized territories is difficult because we lack details about the ancient eras. Yet the entries for subjects like "Hedge," "Boundary," and "Frontier" in the *Dictionary of German Superstitions** furnish an enormous amount of data for more recent times, which can be neither new nor the result of chance, but must have its roots in much older beliefs. We have already seen that certain forms of establishing boundaries—furrows, hedges—can be understood as the materialization of religious borders since sanctuaries were encircled by low stone walls and bushes when the natural space—a clearing or island, for example—did not clearly mark a border.

There is a group of legends common to all of Europe that is worth considering in this regard. We find everywhere the legend of the dishonest surveyor who has stolen land from its legitimate owner by establishing false boundaries, and similarly widespread are the stories about greedy peasants who move border markers to their neighbors' detriment. In both cases the punishment is the same: they are condemned to wander

---

*[*Handwörterbuch des deutschen Aberglaubens,* a large encyclopedia of Germanic folklore. —*Trans.*]

endlessly after death carrying the illegally relocated boundary marker on their backs and asking everyone they meet: "Where should I put this?" They are only freed from their torment on the day someone answers: "Back where you took it from!" The considerable number of accounts of this legend clearly shows that boundary markers have an ancient and profound significance—one which we shall attempt to discover.

The boundary markers of Roman fields (*termini*) were placed under the aegis of the god Terminus, in whose honor the *Terminalia* festival was celebrated. This took place in February and was marked with the sacrifice of a lamb; it therefore had a pronounced sacred character. The *Silvanus orientalis* was also responsible for watching over borders and he was placed in a *lucus* at the edge of the field.* During the Middle Ages, there were different methods for marking property lines. Borders were indicated by boundary markers, or by a furrow for which the dirt pile on the side formed the simulacrum of an encircling wall, or by hedges. The inner space could be marked off by low stonewalls, especially within the proximity of buildings. Trees were marked in forest domains. According to a German charter from 1155, boundary markers bore the sign of the moon in the Rhineland.[1]

In Rhetia, the boundary sign was put on vertical boulders. In ancient Swedish law, it required at least two boundary markers or stakes called *ra* (*staka ok sten ma ra kalla*). To demarcate a path and a field, three were called for. An estate (*tompt*) required five arranged in such a way that one was in the center and the other four encircled it. Jacob Grimm notes that in Iceland and Norway these stones are called *lýrittar* (also spelled *lírittar, lærittar*) and considered sacred. It was next to them, for example, that oaths were sworn (*lýrittar eiðr*). Trees were frequently marked with a cross and rocks were arranged alongside them (*ubi cruces in arbore et lapides subtus infigere jussimus*). This mark is

---

*One wonders if the "fabricated images or idols dedicated to a demon" (*simulacra constructa vel idola daemoni dedicate*) mentioned in a decree of Childebert I from circa 554 (MGH, SS V, 812) might not simply be boundary markers as they refer to the gods under whose protection the estate and its fields are placed.

called *lah* in Old High German (*vulgo lachus appellatur sive divisio*) as is shown by documents dating from 770.

The fixation of borders was a solemn act in which the elders and the *optimates* took part, and it was designated by the verbs *circumducere*, *peragrare*, and *cavallicare* (Old German *pireisa, lantleita, underganc, umbeganc*), which indicated it was accompanied by a circumambulation. The boundary line of the estate being established was followed on foot or horseback. Such trees and stones were sacred and not to be touched. No one had the right, for example, to cut the smallest branch from a marked tree, nor to move the boundary stones of the fields when plowing them. Whoever committed such an impious act would have their head cut off with a plow blade after being buried in the ground up to the neck. Near Hagelsberga in Västmanland (central Sweden) there stands a hill topped by a stone surrounded by a low wall that is called the Chamber of the Nisse (*Tomtenissens stuga*). A spirit could be seen there at night, but it always vanished at daybreak when it heard the bells of Odensvi.

In Lithuania, borders seem to have been placed under the protection of the deity Veliona, also called *Ezagulis,* the "God who lives at the border of the cultivated fields" (*ežia* being the word for a furrow bordering a field).[2] Several traditions also make Perkūnas the guardian of various borders and boundaries. Paul Sébillot points out that the megaliths in France have played the role of boundary markers and have been cited as such in documents. He mentions the *Petra quae vertitur* (Stone that turns) in Berry (thirteenth century) and notes that this name refers to a folk belief. He also mentions the *duo lapides erecti* (two upright stones) that served as the boundaries of the kingdom of Arles and thinks they could be identical to the standing stones of Simandre, France (IV, 1). Stones like this were objects of worship and were even sometimes given offerings and prayers.

In medieval romances, the areas by boundary markers—sometimes replaced by crosses—were always hazardous areas and signals of peril; they were *loca incerta,* meaning that belief in the presence of supernatural beings survived there. I will take three examples attesting to the recuperation of these realities. In Chrétien's *Perceval, the Story of the Grail,* Gawain is lost and meets a wounded knight who tells him to go no further on that road:

> *because that's the boundary of Galvoie*
> *That knights cannot pass*
> *And ever return again.* (6602–4)

The boundary marker therefore signifies, to some extent, the beginning of a journey of no return. In the *Second Continuation of the Story of the Grail,* a "pillar" appears that causes death by a melancholic illness in whoever dares approach too near, one means of indicating that to do this is a sacrilege (31583ff). A Christianized standing stone is also mentioned: on Mount Dolorous there stands a pillar—the word denotes a standing stone—that Merlin placed there at an earlier time. It is surrounded by fifteen crosses, and an *anemi,* meaning a demon, is imprisoned inside it. If anyone asks it: "Who is there?" he will lose his memory and go mad, no matter how wise and shrewd he was before (963ff).

In the Anglo-Norman romance *Gui de Warewic* (Guy of Warwick), written between 1232 and 1242, an *estrange et faé** land called "Ardenne le Grant" appears (12223ff).[3] A fairy knight dwells in this forest around which he had placed enchanted and deadly boundaries. Whoever crosses these borders never returns (*ja mais arere ne repairast;* 12242). Friends of the Muntaigne have gone beyond them and disappeared. Raimbrun, son of Guy, sets off to learn what became of them. He makes his way to the forest, passes by the *mercs periluus,* and afterward reaches a mountain where doors stand open before him. After making the sign of the cross he goes through them. The doors shut behind him and he walks half a league in the darkness where he spies a light and makes his way

*[Strange and fay —*Trans.*]

to a river bordering a moor. This moor surrounds a magnificent castle where time has been suspended:

> *this palace such virtue had:*
> *That a man within would age not a day*
> *Though a thousand years should pass,*
> *Even the eldest would never be taken.*

Here, the boundaries demarcate the Other World, a space that no one can leave unless it is the will of its ruler. The original custom seems to have been reversed here to fit the needs of the story: it is no longer the human beings who are establishing boundaries that will keep the spirits at bay; it is the fairy knight who is protecting himself from humans this way.

A study ought to be undertaken of all the crosses that are erected here and there throughout the rural regions and act as boundary markers at the same time they seek to Christianize these areas, as well as of all the mysterious chapels that are home to strange manifestations, often of a sort quite at odds with what might be expected from a holy site. This goes beyond the scope of the present book, but I point it out as a very useful avenue for future research because the countryside is inseparable from the chivalrous adventure and it can even be asserted that a specific place calls upon a specific knight to perform a specific deed—in fact this task is even reserved for him alone.

15

The Enclosed Space
Is Sacred

An unmistakable sign indicating the sacred character of a place is the fact that it is enclosed, even if this enclosure is strictly symbolic. The Romans made sure that a spot struck by lightning would be surrounded by a wall, and none were allowed to walk there. The sacred groves or woods of the ancient Germans formed a closed spaced, and Thietmar of Merseberg seems to consider "the large, intact, and venerable forest" that surrounds the pagan temple of Riedegost a frontier, an enclosure.[1]

The Gotland laws (*Gutalagen*) prohibit: "sacrifices of all kinds, as well as all the old pagan customs. May no one invoke groves, mounds, pagan gods, sanctuaries, or enclosed spaces . . . with food or drink" (§4). The Christian laws of the Gulathing make the same proscription. In the *Saga of the Gotlanders* it is written that "Before this time and subsequently long after, men worshipped woods and mounds, sanctuaries, and enclosed spaces."[2]

Saint Óláf's Saga reports that during an expedition in Bjarmaland, when Thórir attacked a village, he told his men: "In this enclosure is a mound, and in it is gold and silver all mixed up with earth. Let us go at it. But inside the yard stands the god of the Permians who is called Jómali. Let no one be so bold as to plunder him."[3] When a pagan sanctuary was destroyed on the orders of King Edwin of Northumbria, he explicitly commanded that the hedge encircling it be removed (*destruere fanum cum omnibus septis*). In the Truel parish (Lozère), in the Jonte Valley, the site of Saint Gervais and Saint Protais includes a chapel, hermitage, and an enceinte wall. In the romance of *Perceforest* (fourteenth century) we find a fine example of how these beliefs can survive or be assimilated: the unknown temple stands atop a hill called Mount of the Marvel, in a clearing surrounded by dense thorn bushes, and it is round.

If we refer to the mythology of the ancient Scandinavians—or more specifically, to their cosmogony—we see that the earth consists of three self-contained zones: Asgard, home of the gods; Midgard, the world of men; and Utgard, the dwelling place of the giants, which is to say that of the hostile forces of chaos. Extending all around the world is the ocean in which the Midgard Serpent (*Miðgarðsormr*) lives. The coherence of the whole edifice is ensured vertically, by Yggdrasill, the cosmic tree, and horizontally by the Midgard Serpent, sometimes called the "bond of the earth." The apocalypse (*Ragnarök*) occurs when all these bonds vanish and the forces of chaos, no longer hindered by any barrier, set off to attack the world of the gods.

It should be noted, in passing, that the three enclosures of the world are compound words including *garðr,* a word that means fence and is indicative of the sacred. It so happens that *garðr* (*Gart* in German) goes back to the Indo-European root *gherdh* that means "to weave, to bind." The *garðr* is therefore the concrete and simultaneously religious bond that maintains the cohesion of the domain and the family seat, the center of judicial and cult activities. The *Dísablót* sacrifice to the female spirits (*dísir*) was performed in the home, as was the *álfablót,* the sacrifice addressed to the elves. It was an act of sacrilege to attack the *garðr*—one capable of sparking an act of vengeance in response, as occurs in the *Saga of Víga Glúm* (chap. 7). The universe was therefore organized around a series of concentric circles—enclosures—whose center is the family hearth.

It is especially important to avoid falling into the belief that this vision of the world was restricted to the ancient Germans. Fabienne Cardot has shown that space in Carolingian Austrasia was sometimes perceived as a series of concentric spheres, the smallest consisting of the *villa,* the *pagus,* and the *civitas,* which, with the *vicus* and the *castrum,* were the fundamental frameworks of everyday space. The *loca pagana* were found on the margins of this space.

The ancient Anglo-Saxon laws say that every sanctuary was surrounded by a *friþgeard.* A *garðr* was constructed around all ancient Germanic places that were considered sacred, such as a spring, tree, or fields. These places were designated as *hörgr* in Norse and *harug* in Old High German, meaning "sanctuary, place of worship." According to Jonas of Bobbio, the Lombards had a wooden temple (*fanum*) near Tortona surrounded by trees (*Vita Columbani,* bk. 2, chap. 25).

What was the first thing to occur once one had settled in a space? A fence called a *skíðgarðr* or *stafgarðr* would be built, which by its very nature indicated the sacred nature of the enclosed space, a sanctity that was most likely extended to the occupants of the space. In fact, the proscription of a man sought to expel him from his domain, thereby stripping him of his sacred nature (*mannhelgi*), which means to make him *óheilagr,* "devoid of sacred nature."

The fact that this sacred nature stems from his bonds with the land and with his home clearly emerges from the story of Örn. According to the *Book of Settlements,* "He was condemned in such way that he lost all inviolability at the hands of the sons of Örnund if they found him anywhere outside Vælugerði or within a bowshot of his property" (S 348). It can therefore be seen that the sacred nature of the property marked off by a *garðr* extended to within a bowshot of that boundary, something the Norse designated by the term *örskotshelgi,* a compound of *örskot,* "arrow-shot," and *helgi,* "sacred."

Archaeology has revealed that sites of worship in the medieval West—Old English *ealh/alh, baro, hearg;* Norse *lundr, vé;* and Old High German *baro, harug, loh*—are enclosed spaces, and when it involves a forest, it is also an enclosed space or clearing that is only entered on certain occasions. Recall what Tacitus said in his *Germania* about the worship of Nerthus taking place within a holy grove situated on an island (chap. 40, 3) and the sacred grove of the Semnones, which "no one enters unless bound by a shackle, as an inferior who makes manifest the might of the divine" (chap. 39, 2).[4] The island in the river or the sea is an identical twin of the forest clearing. The *Lex Ripuaria* (Legal Code of the Ripuarian Franks) stipulates that oaths must be sworn "in the hazel grove" (*in araho jurare*), and in Old German the word *forst* ("forest, wood") designates the spot where the tribunal convenes. Hincmar of Reims mentions oaks in 877; the legal texts say "beneath the linden or next to it" (in 1258 and 1261), and it should not be forgotten that the gods of the Scandinavian pantheon gathered beneath the ash tree, Yggdrasill—the cosmic tree.

According to the ninth-century German poem *Muspilli,* the placement of the tribunal (*mahalstat*) had to be marked off (*kimarchôt*), and the same was true for the ancient Scandinavians who called this spot *dómhringr,* the "judgment circle." This location was described as a "most sacred place" (*helgistaðr mikill*), because it is demarcated by "sacred bonds" (*vébönd,* singular *véband*). The Thing, the assembly of free men where lawsuits are judged, is surrounded by hazel stakes, between which a rope is strung (*Egil's Saga,* chap. 56). It so happens that *vé* means "sanctuary"—it is cognate with the Old Saxon word *wîh,* "temple"—and *bönd* means both "bonds" and "deities" (because gods are seen as "binding ones"). The stakes, connected by a rope to form an enclosed area, were called *septa judicalia* in 1283 and *rihtepale* in Middle High German, meaning "legal stakes."

For duels (*holmgangr*), which originally took place on a small island (*holmi* or *holmr*)—and are also a frequent element in medieval romances—a space would be marked off with hazel staffs and an animal sacrifice to the gods would be made before the combat (*Gisla saga,* chap. 2). Sometimes the sacrifice (*blótnaut*) took place after the combat (*Heiðarvíga saga,* chap. 4). The stakes marking off the space are called *tjösnur,* singular *tjasna* (*Kormáks saga,* chap. 10 and 23), and the sacrifice was sometimes made to them as indicated by the word *tjösnublót,* "sacrifice to the stakes, to the boundary markers." In the Middle High German poem the *Nibelungenlied,* oaths are still sworn within a circle.

The preceding should leave no doubt about the sacred nature of all spaces that have been enclosed or given some kind of boundary. We could add to these examples those of the otherworldly castles surrounded by a magical barrier. I am thinking in particular of the enchanter Malduk's castle in Ulrich von Zatzikhoven's *Lanzelet,* which is bordered by a malefic marsh. In the same text, the home of the "water nymph" who kidnapped Lanzelet as a child is a round crystal island. In the work of Chrétien de Troyes, we have the adventure of the Joy of the Court (in *Erec et Enide*), which suggests the same theme. It is an orchard enclosed by a wall of clouds (or air), where lives a very simplified sort of fairy and a knight, Mabonagrain, who possesses all the characteristics of a giant.

Formation of the Domain of Lusignan.
Illustration from Thüring von Ringoltingen's version of
Melusine. *Strassburg: Knoblochtzer, ca. 1478.*

16

The Contract
with the Spirits

Once the domain has been marked out, it remains to build the living quarters and farm buildings, but one can never be entirely certain that all the local spirits have been dispersed, nor even certain that the sanctification and the patronage of the gods one worships is going to be more powerful than the powers wielded by these spirits. Cohabitation will therefore be arranged and a tacit contract with these spirits shall be drawn up. Depending on the nature of the space, the country, and the kinds of constructions, this contract can take a variety of forms.

Almost everywhere until fairly recent times, we find confirmation of the existence of the rite of sacrificing a living being in order to be able to erect a building. Folklorists and ethnologists have long interpreted this rite as a sacrifice addressed to the local land spirits so they will not oppose the construction. In fact, this sacrifice appears like a payment of damages for the land being occupied. The individual pays his due to the land spirit in order to be able to establish the hegemony of agriculture over wild nature.

We are poorly informed about ancient times, and with the Greeks and Romans, for example, the authors are revealingly terse and only mention the rites.[1] Herodotus speaks this way about the founding of a city by Darius, who did so without respecting the rites and consulting the oracles. Herodotus considers this an impious action. Vitruvius, when mentioning something under construction, speaks of the "respect for traditions." A Roman legend tells how a crack appeared in the walls of the *Forum Romanum* and could not be closed until after Curtius was rushed there with his horse. A Greek legend informs us that a yong girl was immured within the foundation of Antiochia and another was treated the same way during the construction of the city's large theater. Moreover, archaeologists have found skeletons in the walls of buildings built between 2500 and 2000 BCE. Among the ancient Egyptians, the sacrifice of young men and women, and prisoners, appears to have been common practice when the first stone of a public building was laid. We should note that this rite also appears in the Bible:

> Cursed be the man before the Lord, that riseth up and buildeth this city Jericho: he shall lay the foundation thereof in his firstborn, and in his youngest son shall he set up the gates of it. (Joshua 6:26, KJV)

To the best of my knowledge, the oldest medieval account can be found in Nennius's *Historia Brittonum* (chap. 40–42), written around 966. This is the story of the tower of King Vortigern (Breton: Guorthigirn; Vertigier in the Round Table romances), which is famous on account of its connection to the legend of Merlin the Enchanter.[2] Because the tower collapsed every night, the king consulted seers who arrived at the conclusion that in order for it to remain standing, it was necessary to sacrifice a fatherless child. The child selected was Marlin Ambrosius, but he managed to get out of this unenviable position by revealing that two dragons were lying at the chosen spot and that they should be allowed to escape from this place where they seemed to be held prisoner. I will pass over the allegorical interpretation of these dragons, which is dependent on ancient Celtic and biblical traditions (Esther 10:7 and 11:6), and instead take up Alexander H. Krappe's interpretation. He clearly demonstrated that what is at work here involves the exploitation of the theme of sacrificing a human being to appease a genius loci that often adopted the form of a serpent, dragon, or lizard.

In an ancient Celtic tale called *Lludd and Llefelys* we find the prehistory, so to speak, of the dragons described by Nennius. Three scourges afflicted the isle of Britain, the second of which was a loud screech that could be heard over every household on May Day Eve. This cry caused sterility in animals, trees, lands, and waters, and caused pregnant women to abort. The source of this cry was a dragon fighting against a "dragon of a foreign race." Llefelys's counsels for getting rid of this plague are quite interesting and I have italicized the important passages:

> After thou hast returned home, cause the Island to be measured in its length and breadth, and in the place where thou dost find *the exact central point,* there cause a pit to be dug, and cause a cauldron full of the best mead that can be made to be put in the pit, with a covering of satin over the face of the cauldron. And then, in thine own person do thou remain there watching, and thou wilt see the dragons fighting in the form of terrific animals. And at length they will take the form of dragons in the air. And last of all, after wearying themselves with fierce and furious fighting, they will fall in the form of two pigs upon the covering, and they will sink in, and the covering with them, and they will draw it down to the very bottom of the cauldron. And they will drink up the whole of the mead; and after that they will sleep. Thereupon do thou immediately fold the covering around them, and bury them in a kistvaen, in the strongest place thou hast in thy dominions, and hide them in the earth. *And as long as they shall bide in that strong place no plague shall come to the Island of Britain from elsewhere.*[3]

What we see here is the first dragon, the form of the territory's guardian spirit, under attack by a foreign monster disputing it for sovereignty. The advice provided by Llewelys is enlightening because it does not seek to kill the beasts—quite the contrary! It is necessary to bury the two dragons so they can thenceforth protect the region. Thus he seeks to divert their energy, or, if you prefer, to return them to their primordial duty. Furthermore, the fact that they can only be captured at the island's central point is quite revealing; among the Celts the theme of the center goes hand in hand with the sanctity of places. Every center is sacred.[4]

While medieval accounts are rare, there are many examples from more recent times. In 1792, Michel Popoff spoke of a child walled up in the foundations of a Russian city. In Romania, the legend of Master Manole is centered on the theme of a human sacrifice necessary for the construction of a monastery.[5] Throughout the Slavic world similar stories about towns (Scutari) and churches (Curtea de Arges; Trei Ierarhi) are widespread. In Barcelona, Spain, Poblet Monastery and Holy Cross Hospital were only built, according to legend, after a sacrifice had been made for the construction. In Värmland, Sweden, the man or animal (often a sow) sacrificed during the construction of a church becomes the tutelary spirit of the place (*kyrkrå* or *kyrkgrimen*) responsible for maintaining the site's sanctity and keeping watch over it.[6] In Finland it is also said: "In every church a *kirkrå* can be found; it is the first person to have been buried in this spot." The same claim is made there for cemeteries. Around 1600, Johannes Bureus indicates that there is a kind of plate on the church of Sigtuna, Sweden, where those who move about at night leave a little food to ensure that the *rå* does no harm to travelers.

In France, Paul Sébillot mentions the bridges of Rosporden (Finistère) that will only remain standing once a child has been walled inside the bridge support. Custom claims that at another bridge, near Pontivy, a person was buried beneath the first piling.[7] Sébillot also recalls that a cat was found that had been buried alive in the walls of Saint Germain Castle when the castle was built in 1547, a euphemized version of the original rite. When the old Blackfriar Bridge was demolished in London in March of 1867, bones were found beneath its foundations, and on June 15, 1871, Lord Leigh was accused of having walled up one to eight innocents in the foundations of a bridge in Stoneleigh.[8] A more exhaustive search could easily turn up a great many accounts of this nature.

We should also keep in mind that these rites became less barbarous the closer they occur to the modern era. Animals replaced men before being replaced by their blood, which in turn was replaced by wine. Subterfuge was even used: an individual's shadow was measured and its measurement was placed in the foundations. However, when we know that the shadow is one of the individual's doubles (alter egos), it is easy to see that it is a form of human sacrifice transposed onto a symbolic level.[9]

Several clues in the northern Germanic regions allow us a glimpse of other forms of the contract, which are confirmed by folk traditions that were still flourishing in the nineteenth century. It seems that a place was reserved for the spirits within the immediate proximity of the house; in other words, an alliance was formed with them. Most of the time these were stones or trees to which oblations were made. In the *Kristni saga* (Story of Conversion) we read:

> At Giljá there stood a stone to which he [Koðrán] and his kinsmen used to sacrifice, and they claimed that their guardian spirit (*ármaðr*) lived in it. Koðrán said that he would not have himself baptised until he knew who was more powerful, the bishop or the spirit in the stone. After that, the bishop went to the stone and chanted over it until the stone burst apart. Then Koðrán thought he understood that the spirit had been overcome. Koðrán then had himself and his whole household baptised. . . .[10]

The text speaks for itself as it clearly shows that Koðrán dreaded the wrath of the spirit protecting his farm and wanted to be certain that God could protect him if he chose to worship him. In the *Tale of Thorvald Far-Traveler,* there is also a spirit called "prophet, seer" (*spámaðr*) who lives in a stone and offers advice (chap. 2).[11] Numerous more recent accounts corroborate that offerings were made to land spirits living beneath stones. A peasant of Sönderstrup (Denmark) owned a spirit. He left gruel near the stone for it. When his son saw this, he asked him what he was doing. His father told him: "It is for the *gaardbo*." The son overturned the stone and found congealed blood beneath it. The next day, the farmer's best cow was found strangled in the barn. Near the Omland farm in Fjotland parish (Norway), a large stone could be seen that had a large crack. The local folk placed food and drink in this crack on Christmas Eve.[12]

Waldemar Liungman, who has exhaustively studied the *numens* connected to places,[13] discovered the same phrase in two manuscripts written in Old Swedish: *tomta gudhane,* "the gods of the building site." The first, the *Själinna thröst* (Comfort of the Soul), involves a woman who, following the meal, would set the table for these creatures while saying that if they came to eat, her livestock would prosper and all would go well. In the second, which contains the Revelations of Saint Brigitte (*Birgittas uppenbarelser*), priests forbid this kind of worship of the *tompta gudhi* as it seems to threaten their right to a tithe in livestock, bread, wine, and natural goods. In both cases, it is impossible to know precisely if we are dealing with land spirits (*tomta rå*) or household spirits (*gårdsrå*).

These spirits are guarantors for the prosperity of the estate and are already in the immediate proximity of household spirits. When the inhabitants of the house adopt them, or vice versa, the genii loci become guardians of the hearth, but it would be inaccurate to claim this is always the case because the tutelary spirit could also be the house's former owner, who, after his death, was buried beneath the hearth or the threshold. However, I believe we need to pay close attention to where the spirit resides within the demarcated space. The household spirit lives inside the house, often near the fireplace or hearth; the land spirit lives outside. Whichever case it may be, I can also suggest as a hypothesis that the adoption of a spirit and its introduction into the house is a countermeasure intended to foil the intrigues of the genii loci.

At the end of the sixteenth century, Lasicius speaks of the *Barstucci* (*Barstukai*) in his essay on the *Gods of the Samogitians* (chap. 47). He likens them to dwarves (*Barstuccas quos Germani erdmenlin, hoc est subterraneos, vocant*) and calls them servants of the god Piutscetum, protector of sacred groves and trees (*qui sacris arboribus et luci praeest*).[14] Matthäus Prätorius (sixteenth century) gives us a glimpse of how the "specialists," pagan priests called Kaukuczones or Barztukkones, were capable of enchanting the *Barstucci/erdmenlin* (chthonic creatures) to settle in this place or that. This is a good example of taming local land spirits and transforming them into household spirits.

A tree often stands right next to the main house in the Scandinavian countries. This tree is frequently a birch and is reputedly the home of the land spirit. The most common name for this spirit is *gardvord,* formed from *gard,* meaning "wall, boundary," and later "estate"; and *vord,* meaning "guardian." The tree is called *boträ* (*bosträd*), *vårdträd* (the "*vord*-tree"), as well as *tomteträd* and *tuntré.* This tree can be an oak, birch, elder, or elm and is considered to be the totem tree on which the family fortunes depend (Sweden), and the dwelling place of the *tomtegubbe,* another name for the land spirit. Offerings of food were placed at its feet and its roots were sometimes watered with milk.[15]

To facilitate understanding of this presentation, I would like to briefly recall the names of the spirits connected with farms in the Scandinavian countries:

Denmark: *Nisse, Lille Niels, Nis, Nis Puge, Puge, gaardbo, gaardbonisse, gaardbuk* (the "dweller in the estate").

Norway: *Tuss(e), Bokke, Tomtegubbe, Tuftefolk (-bonde, -gubbe, -kall), Tunkall, Tunvord* (the "guardian of the garden"), *gardvord* ("guardian of the estate"), *gardsbonde* ("dweller in the estate"), *haugbonde* ("mound dweller").

Sweden: *Vätte, Yomtegubbe (-bise)* (the "dweller in the estate"), *Tomtkall* (the "Old Man of the Estate"), *Niss, Goanisse* (the "Good Nisse").

There is an oak in Bö, Norway, at whose foot the *haugbonde* (dweller of the mound or hill) is propitiated with gruel on Christmas Day. If the plate was found empty the next day, good fortune was certain for the farmer's cows and horses. We should note, incidentally, that similar offerings can be found almost everywhere. In the Telemark region of Norway offerings were made to the *Vätter* (spirits) on hills called *Vättehauge*. In West Bothnia (Västerbotten) coins were offered to the *Vitra;* in Funen, the fishermen do the same for the water spirits (*sjörå*), and when fording a river a coin is tossed to the undine (*Aamand,* meaning "river person").

It is therefore easy to see that the obvious purpose of all these rites is to neutralize or attract the favors of local spirits so they may be transformed into guardian powers. The farm and its inhabitants' prosperity in fact depends on the moods of said spirits, so it is sometimes necessary to renew the signs of esteem or worship at regular intervals, most often once a year at Christmas. This date, which marks the time of omens and thereby heralds the coming year, was certainly not chosen at random. The Cycle of Twelve Days (from Christmas to Epiphany) corresponds to the famous Epagomenal Days, a period that does not belong to either the year that is ending or the coming year. It is a "no man's time" that represents a moment when the Other World is open and when the spirits can roam freely over the earth and are therefore particularly dreadful. It should also be kept in mind that before the conversion to Christianity in Iceland, the ancient pagan Yule festivities also had associations with the "sacrifice to the elves" (*álfablót*).

The offerings are also a kind of compensation given to the spirits whose lands have been taken. People must live in symbiosis with them if they wish to prosper, and it is even necessary to avoid adopting Christianity because it drives them away. Many legends have as their theme the departure of the "dwarves," the "silent people," the local land spirits, who cannot stand the noise of the bells of the recently built churches.

I should also say a word about the building legends in which men are compelled to turn to a supernatural being (giant, devil) in order to erect a bridge over a fast-moving river. The wondrous assistant always demands as payment the life or soul of the first living thing to cross the bridge, which is nothing more nor less than a sacrifice *a posteriori*. In fact, the devil, the most frequent form this assistant takes, shows himself to be stronger than the spirit of the waters and manages to build the bridge. However, he is always foiled, since the humans always release a cat or rooster as a true substitute for the sacrifice expected by the builder.

We could take the interpretation further and ask ourselves whether the devil in question was not simply the genius loci who first manifests by creating an obstacle to the construction, and then by negotiating a contract with the humans—a contract that requires the sacrifice of a life? This is the price demanded for any encroachment on its territory. Whichever of these two interpretations may be true, they are part of the same continuum and there is every reason to believe that the Christian forms of these legends featuring the appearance of a demon are only representations of an older belief in which the spirit has to receive what is owed to it.

17

The Circular and the Rectangular

A Hypothesis

One of the intrinsic difficulties in a study of local land spirits is the identification of what could be called their sanctuary. Is this place—boundary marker, tree, spring, and so on—under the patronage of a god or spirit? This is a fundamental question, but one that is very difficult to answer today due to a painful lack of the elements needed to make such an evaluation. The following analysis, based on the comparative method—which alone seems capable of advancing any kind of theory—should fall under the heading of conjecture rather than certainty.

For the pagans of the Middle Ages there were two kinds of religious structures: some are round; the others are square or rectangular. The same thing can be observed throughout the Indo-European world, and this has been the case since classical antiquity. Georges Dumézil and other researchers have exhaustively studied this point, so I am using ~~rch as a starting point.[1]

guishes a Roman temple (*templum*) from a simple reli-
(*aedes*) is the shape that is directly determined by its
To establish a temple, the auguries were consulted and

122

then the regions of the heavens were marked off with a curved staff.*
Moreover, the auguries free the plot of land and declare it empty
(*liberare, effari*), and then the sides of the temple are drawn. Here is
how Karl Joachim Marquardt explains the inauguration:

> The site's boundaries are determined by the auguries then estab-
> lished by a solemn declaration (*quibusdam conceptis verbis*). It is then
> called *locus effatus* and it is used to determine the shape of the build-
> ing to be erected upon it. This is a square or rectangle whose four
> sides correspond with the four cardinal points. The frontispiece,
> in accordance with old Roman custom, runs along the west side so
> that whoever sacrifices a burnt offering at the altar in front of the
> temple, and who is looking at the image of the god in the open *cella*,
> is facing east.[2]

The orientation of the celestial *templum* is fundamentally from west
to east, and the inaugurated site is a symmetrical representation of the
heavens, while whatever is not inaugurated remains essentially of the earth.

By studying the sanctuary of the Vesta, which is an *aedes rotunda,*
Georges Dumézil has shown that the eternal fire burning within it corresponds to the Vedic *gārhapatya,* meaning the "fire of the master of
the house," which is not "intended to receive offerings but to materialize through a hearth the legitimate abode of a man or group of men
on a point of the earth," which requires a round contour.[3] It so happens that Vesta is an earthly deity, she is even the earth insofar as she
supports the life of men, and as such is round, says Festus, and Ovid
asserts that "she is the same thing as the earth."[4]

---

*Similarly, we may note that the pyramids of Egypt are precisely oriented so that their
corners evoke an ideal microcosm. "The four corners of the world (northeast, south-
east, southwest, northwest), governed by the pyramidion, mark out the cardinal regions
(which correspond to each face of the monument). This arrangement brings to mind
the cosmogony . . . in which the 'Great One of the Five,' Osiris (or Geb), considered as
supreme god, occupies the center of a square of four gods over whom he rules" (Isabelle
Franco, *Rites et croyances d'éternité,* 86).

At the conclusion of an important study, Jean-Pierre Vernant states there is every reason to believe that the circle in Greece characterizes those powers that are both chthonic and female, and are connected with the image of Mother Earth. The Earth Mother holds in her womb the dead, the human generations, and plant growth.[5] Now these latter are, in the medieval West, subject to the good will of the dead, and this has caused unending confusion between ancestor worship, worship of Mother Earth, and that of the land spirits who can be taken as manifestations of the dead and of the Great Goddess. A circular building is therefore multivalent.

If we start from the assumption that there was an ancient unity of Indo-European beliefs, we can imagine that similar notions survived in different cultural areas, and likewise a similar opposition between round and rectangular spaces. In the German-Scandinavian region, archaeologists have unearthed the substructures of sanctuaries that allow the ground plan to be drawn. These buildings were parallelograms, squares, or rectangles, and the orientation of their walls corresponded, within a few degrees, to the cardinal points. They therefore closely match what we have found in Rome and are clearly placed at the point where the earth meets the sky. This is the case with Sæból, Rútsstaðir, and Ljárskógar.[6] The *Kjalnesinga saga* (Saga of the People of Kjalarnes) describes a temple to Thor that measured twenty feet long by sixty feet wide, but the interior was round!

The Scandinavian sanctuary or temple was called *hof.* It was rectangular and in Norway, for example, it consisted of two rooms. One was oblong or approximately rectangular and called the *skáli.* It took up two-thirds of the building and was the site of the sacrificial banquets. The other room was called the *afhús;* it was square and was probably where the pagan altar stood.[7] Researchers have noted that the proportions of the *skáli* and the *afhús* were the same as those of the naves and choirs of the small Norwegian wood or stone churches.

In Iceland, based on the excavations undertaken at the sites of Ytri-Fagradalur and Hvammur, the oldest form of the sanctuary seems to have been circular. On the other hand, the sanctuaries of the continental

Germanic peoples during the Bronze Age were small square buildings. The permanent coexistence of circular and rectangular sanctuaries seems probable, which some researchers have interpreted in the following way: the gods of the Vanir were worshipped in the one, and Aesir deities in the other.

As a correlation of the postulate stated above regarding the original unity of ancient Indo-European beliefs, we can posit that circular sites—meaning those whose circularity is primarily the work of man, and whose sacred character is evident—are not dedicated to the

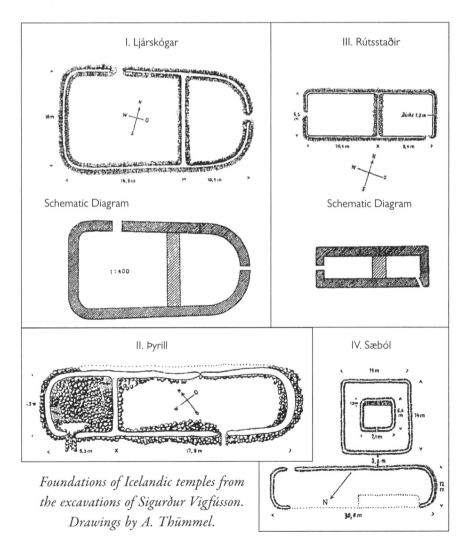

Foundations of Icelandic temples from the excavations of Sigurður Vigfússon. Drawings by A. Thümmel.

inaccessible and remote high gods of the pantheon but to the local land spirits who are so close to men and play such a huge role in their affairs. Thus, these trees, wells, or stones surrounded by hedges or a low wall would be the sanctuaries of the essentially earthbound genii loci, as indicated by their circular outline.

A second point enables us to further refine this hypothesis. The gods' sanctuaries are never far from the home; among the ancient Scandinavians they even share the same roof. Consequently, we ought to be able to precisely situate the aforementioned forest or agrarian sanctuaries on a map, but the mere fact that they are at a distance from habitations and villages offers us a valuable clue about their nature.

Let us recall what is consistently stated in the sermons, counciliar decrees, and penitientials: they inform us that people made their way to remote places to visit trees, stones, and springs. This would therefore not seem to be worship of gods from the Germanic pantheon but rather a cult directed at land spirits. In the current stage of my research I am unfortunately unable to develop this hypothesis further. Further research will be necessary to refute or confirm it.

18

The Conquest of the Space

Once the estate has been marked out and the house and farm buildings built, the need to protect them still remains, and then one would set off conquering space that is yet unclaimed. Enclosures are established, first that of the *tún,* the garden, directly adjacent to the main house. This is a primal sacred space where the tree of the spirit (*túntré*) stands and where a sacred animal—often a pig—is raised. It will be sacrificed on Jól (Christmas) to the god Freyr (third function). The act of colonizing, which takes place under the aegis of an antagonistic sacred power, can only be achieved through acknowledgment of the genius loci, a recognition marked by a sanctuary and worship. It transforms the spirit into a guardian power. Once this has been achieved, the colonization of the space has also been completed.

We ought to also discuss the home as a sacred space in which the threshold, the hearth, and the main roof beam play an important role, but this would take us beyond the scope of the present study. I will simply say that during the thirteenth century when moving into a new home, the residents would bury at the four corners of the house a pot holding a variety of things for the household spirits. In more recent times, four consecrated branches would be buried at the four corners of the future house before construction began.

The colonization of the surrounding area was mounted from the home and the farmed land. Its principal characteristic seems to be a particular structuring of the space, which was realized in stages. First, more or less temporary installations were created, surrounded by a hedge or some other kind of fence, and this concerned not only pieces of land but also trees and springs. An enclosed space of this type is called a *hörgr* in Old Norse, which can be loosely translated as "worship place, sanctuary," a name that suggests these are spots from which the local land spirits have been expelled. They are a kind of refuge offering safety and protection from the spirits and from other human beings. As a general rule, Christians initially set up crosses at these spots, replacing one form of the sacred with another. Since the fields were often far from the farm, it was necessary when visiting them to cross through "unsure territories" in which it would be necessary to establish some safe havens. It was also necessary to protect these pastures and meadows against intrusion by any untamed land spirits.* These spots were thus placed under the patronage and protection of a deity. Jan de Vries has drawn

---

*There is a passage in William of Auxerre's *De universo* (bk. III, XXIV) that clearly states that places colonized by man are sanctified: "*It is even told how someone, on seeing an army of this kind [the army in question is the Mesnie Hellequin, the spectral Wild Hunt], was terror struck and fled from the public road to find a haven in the neighboring field. He remained unscathed while this army traveled past him, and suffered no harm from any of these knights. The reason for this is that many believe that **the fields enjoy the protection of the Creator** because of their usefulness to mankind. This is the reason why evil spirits have no access to them, nor do they have the power to harm any people they find on them. Of course, the horde of idolaters would attribute this protection and defense, while admitting that they believe in it and have heard speak of it, to **the sacred nature of these plowed fields**. And if one of these folk impelled by terror went into these fields, he would believe he was not trying to hide in a meadow but was placing himself under **the protection and authority of said sacred signs. I think they believe that it would be Ceres, the goddess of the fields, who would have protected the man taking this action** and that this army could cause no harm to anyone who found himself within the boundaries of the kingdom of Ceres.*" I have put the most significant passages in bold type. If we replace the phrase "evil spirits" with "local land spirits" in William's text—in other words, if we eliminate the Christian interpretation—it becomes apparent that the earth on which man settles is sacred.

up a fairly long list of theophoric names in which the gods Odin, Ullr, Frey, Thor, and Njord are combined with nouns like field, meadow, or island, not to mention the place-names that indicate the presence of a sanctuary, such as *Oslunda, Frölunda* (sacred grove of Odin, or of Freyr, respectively), or even *Närtuna* (Njord's enclosure).[1]

If we do not just focus on the place-names that simply describe a morphogeographical feature of the landscape (such as *Hvitá,* "white river," or *Ljósavatn,* "clear lake") and provide reference points on the paths leading from one point to another, place-names more importantly invest the space with a human presence and expel its natural "wildness." The functions of place-names can be therefore outlined as follows:

1. They establish the boundaries of estates and properties.
2. They serve as the foundation for family or clan identity, given the fact that most often the farm carries the name of its first owner.
3. They indicate which god protects the region.
4. They sometimes refer to the duty of the person living in the space, for example, *Spákonufell,* "Mount of the Seeress."
5. They are part of human memory, as they preserve remembrance of specific events. For example, after Thord's ship was lost with all hands, the place where the keel of his boat was found was named *Kjalarey,* "Keel Island," and the place where the drowned sailors were buried was named *Haugsnes,* "Cape of the Mound."
6. They indicate places with a reputation for being dangerous; for example, *Tröllaskogr,* "Troll Forest."[2]

Thanks to these names, the *terrae incognitae* are gradually claimed; teetering on the border of civilization the unknown lands soon become islands. It is here that the land spirits find refuge and where they continue to dwell. The places that escape human control are quite stereotypical and essentially correspond to lands that are difficult to live in and to cultivate. This therefore causes a new natural distribution of spirits and places based on the inaccessibility of these spaces. So it is perfectly normal that the *loca incerta,* the dangerous places, would be forests, moors, mountains, as well as marshes and—as we shall see—bodies of water in general.

This is something that the medieval romances have preserved best. When knights-errant left the civilized space and plunged into the unknown after crossing through the marches of cultivated lands, they always stumble onto either a bewitching space (*locus amoenus*) where they meet fairies or a place of fear and horror (*locus terribilus*) where they encounter monsters of all kinds: giants, dragons, devils, sirens, women of the wood, and so on. It is almost a certainty that these alarming, monstrous creatures are the fictionalized vision of land spirits who have been here completely transposed into the sphere of the marvelous. I can therefore state that the marvelous rehabilitates and adapts local beliefs, and then, as the literature congeals and fixes such encounters into stereotypes, they are disengaged from their sources to become, in short, nothing more than recreational entertainment and compensatory dreams. But the local land spirits continued to live on in their "new clothes," and it is their survival and resistant capabilities that I will demonstrate next.

Monsters defending Mount Canigou. Illustration from Thüring von Ringoltingen, Melusine. *Basel: Bernhard Richel, ca. 1473.*

PART THREE

Survivals and Transformations

Formation of the Domain of Lusignan.
Illustration from Thüring von Ringoltingen, Melusine.
Basel: Bernhard Richel, ca. 1473.

19

Waters, Springs, and Fountains

Some land spirits are extremely reluctant to leave the domain from which they have been expelled and will seize any opportunity to regain possession of their property. This is implied, without being explicitly stated, in medieval literary descriptions of places haunted by strange manifestations (see part 1 of this book). Some places better than others, however, have resisted the invasion and settlement of men. These include forests, mountains, waters, and more generally places that have been abandoned and returned to nature.

On the fictional level, it seems a literary rehabilitation took place with a fictional transposition and specialization of the spirits that were "adulterated" this way. A connection is established between a personage and a place.[1] This place would be haunted by that subject. This is how the forests became the habitat of beings grouped together under the names of "dwarves" and "giants," and the waters became the home of fairies, sirens, and various disturbing, zoomorphic creatures that recent folk traditions have dubbed with a thousand different names. To review all the places that serve as theaters for manifestations that can be attributed to spirits would require a huge tome, so I will only examine the most impressive of these sites.

We most often meet fairies by the shores of lakes, fountains, or springs, and this is even a constant theme in the stories about Melusine. The co-occurrence of these sites and a lady—regardless of what name she bears—has commanded the attention of researchers who have long realized that fairies could very often be considered as aquatic spirits: an anthropomorphic expression of the *numen* reputed to dwell in such places. Fairies rarely wander far from what clearly seems to be their natural element and Melusine, for example, who Raymondin of Poitiers meets near the Fountain of Thirst, arranges matters so that a spring is included in her husband's future domain.

A passage from the *Lancelot-Grail* offers an interesting observation when Queen Guinevere, wife of King Arthur, reaches the Fountain of the Fairies, so named "because the folk who lived in the forest had seen there several times very beautiful ladies and, knowing nothing of who they might be, said they were fairies" (53, 19).

But while some spirits are definitely aquatic spirits, the syncretic nature of these creatures has conferred upon them a specificity so strong it conceals their origin; all that remains are the springs and fountains near which they like to linger and even dwell.

In the *Elucidation,* the text that serves as an introduction to *Perceval, the Story of the Grail,* we find an explanation for how the kingdom of Logres was destroyed during an earlier time. Here is the gist:

> There were once there many maidens of the wells, that is to say of the springs and fountains, and travelers knew where to find them. They came out of the fountains bearing golden cups and silver and gold bowls, and they gave those passing by whatever they desired to eat and drink. One day, King Amangons raped one and stole her golden cup. His vassals followed his example and the gentle maidens vanished. The land became dry and the kingdom a desert; in short, it henceforth became a wasteland.[2]

These figures were therefore closely connected to the third function as defined by Dumézil: fertility. Moreover, it clearly seems they had power over irrigation of the lands by means of the springs. Their behavior is that of good land spirits who, we note, did not flee the presence of humans. The act of Armangons and his vassals, comparable to a sacrilege, in some way triggered their vengeance—which took the form of desertification. Henceforth the land of this kingdom would be of no use to mankind.

A similar notion can be found in ancient Wales. The *Black Book of Carmarthen,* written around 1200, tells how the king of Dyvet raped a young girl who guarded a magic fountain. The fountain began to swell up and overflowed its borders—its waters drowned sixteen old forts.[3] In this text and in the *Elucidation,* it is completely valid to interpret the consequences of a misdeed as punishment. The land spirit was offended directly in the person of these maidens, or because they were his representatives, and he chastened the criminals with the means at his disposal; in other words, he drove the wicked away and took back possession of his places.

When the spirit assumes the form of a female figure—which is only one among many possibilities—Christianity took full advantage of it, but without totally eradicating the original tone of the belief. In the *Life of Saint Patrick* we find the following incident that is quite revealing and for which I provide a brief summary:

> Two young women, Ethna the Fair and Fedelm the Red Rose, went to a fountain to draw water in Rathcrogan. Saint Patrick conversed with them and gave them such a convincing lesson of catechism that they converted. They received the Eucharist and died forthwith, and were then buried near the fountain.[4]

There could be no clearer way of telling us that these maids were "goddesses" of paganism and very likely the spirits of this fountain. Pierre Bersuire (born at the end of the thirteenth century in

Saint-Pierre-du-Chemin, in the Vendée region, and died in 1362), said in his *Reductorium morale* (XIV, 30) that fairies often haunted lakes. The ancient Slavs called water spirits *vily*, meaning "fairies," and a document of the Bulgarian emperor Constantine Asen (1258–1277) speaks of a "well of the fairies." Pierre Gallais has just recently shown us in a new book that the fountain (or spring) is almost inseparable from the figure of the fairy.[5]

In Walter Map's *De nugis curialium* (II, 11), which he wrote between 1181 and 1193, several legends tell the story of the meeting between a fairy and a mortal, notably that of Wastinius of Wastinog and the lady of the lake of Brecknock. Three nights in a row, Wastinius surprised women dancing in his fields. He pursued them up to a pond in which they vanished. He then heard a voice telling him how he could capture one of these women. He managed to kidnap one whom he wed, but the marriage was subject to a taboo that he did not respect, and the siren returned to the lake with the children they had produced together. Although a variety of traditions are combined and superimposed in this legend—Melusinian prohibition, for example, and the theme of swanwomen[6]—it is easy to recognize ladies of the lake in these mysterious figures otherwise known as land spirits.

It is possible that the plural number of ladies is due to a multiplication of a scholarly or even courtly nature because only one of these creatures plays a role. The others seem to be mentioned merely to confuse the reader and as a derivative of a very widespread motif that maintained fairies practically always come in threes, like the Parcae. Moreover, Laurence Harf-Lancner has clearly shown that this fairy possesses, if we believe the parallel narratives, the form of a horse and that the taboo—to never strike her with a horse's bridle—is intended to conceal her animal nature.[7] Incidentally, I would like to emphasize that horses are one of the most common forms taken by water spirits. In the legend of Wastinius there was therefore, originally, the belief in the existence of such spirits and the possibility of wedding one. The character of the lady of the lake spirit is also shown by the fact she brings her husband happiness and prosperity, just as in all the stories in which man succeeds in obtaining the favor or neutrality of the local spirits.

The *Life of Saint Malo* by the deacon Beli also tells us that the spirit of the place can remain perfectly in the shadows and its existence or presence can only be revealed through deduction, as shown in the following example in which a man of God, following a footpath, makes his way to a fountain of very clear water filled with precious stones that twinkle like stars:

> He lifted his hand and blessed the fountain in the name of the Holy Trinity, and then filled the vessel he carried with water to the very brim. He raised it to his mouth to drink, but was unable to get even a taste of it. He then placed the vessel over his left arm . . . drew water again, with the same result. The third time, he lifted his hand as before and, blessing the fountain, said aloud: "Lord, You who at Horeb caused a sure and steady stream of water to flow from a rock, who gave birth to several rivers for Moses and Aaron and their people when they were almost dying of thirst, give me water from this fountain so that I may bring some to my master, and make it so I may drink some before." He then drew more of this very sweet water for the third time and poured it into his mouth, which he drank, then took with him the water remaining in his vessel. (chap. 20)

Philippe Walter is the first to have glimpsed what lies behind an otherwise seemingly stereotypical hagiographic legend: "It is easy to recognize the Christianizing elements of this wondrous fountain. A kind of taboo is attached to it: no one may drink its water unless certain favorable conditions have been met. Saint Malo, because he was one of God's elect and because he heeded a complete sacramental ritual (blessing, invocation of the Trinity, and so forth), was able to appropriate the dangerous magic of the site and convert it into a divine virtue."[8] In fact, the ritual used is an exorcism whose purpose is not to vanquish the magic of the site but to defeat its land spirit, to neutralize it and thereby

reintegrate the fountain into civilized Christian space. Henceforth, anyone could quench his thirst there. The water that refused to allow itself
to be drunk is a theophany; it displays the presence of a sacred power
that is not that of Christians.

A fountain seen in the *Life of Saint Patrick,* the Irish evangelist,
should be interpreted in similar fashion:

> Patrick went to the fountain of Findmag. Slan [meaning *salutiferum*
> or "salubrious"] was this fountain's name. Patrick was told that the
> pagans *worshipped the fountain like a god.* It so happens that the foun-
> tain was *square* and there was a square stone above it. Saint Patrick
> was jealous on behalf of the living God . . . , and he commanded that
> the stone be raised, and none could do it. But Patrick, with the help
> of Crainnech, whom he had baptized, was able to raise this stone.[9]

I have italicized the important points: the worship of the pagans was
addressed, of course, not to the fountain but to the *numen* that inhabited it; the form of the fountain that clearly indicates it is a sanctuary;
and finally the impossibility for pagans to dislocate and de-sanctify the
site, an action only Christians could achieve successfully because the
Christian faith always prevails over paganism.

The sacred nature of such places that are inhabited and haunted by
a spirit also emerges from a passage in *De mirabilibus Hiberniae* (On
the Wonders of Ireland) by Gerald of Wales:

> There is a fountain in Munster which, being touched or even looked
> at by any human being, will immediately inundate the whole prov-
> ince with rain. Nor will it cease until a priest, specially appointed,
> and who has been pure since birth, has appeased the fountain by
> performing mass in a chapel, which is known to have been founded
> not far off for this purpose, and by sprinkling holy water and the
> milk of a cow having only one color—a rite, indeed, extremely
> barbarous, and void of all reason.[10]

The Christianization of the elements in this story is quite superficial. In fact, touching or even seeing this fountain is a sacrilege that the *numen* punishes by sending rain that only ceases when the restorative rites reestablishing the site's sacredness have been performed. This is obvious as the priest, similar to a vestal, must be pure (virgin), and the cow's single color makes it an uncommon animal that possesses a specific quality expressed by milk, a white liquid, meaning it is pure and primordial. Gerald's observation—"a rite, indeed, extremely barbarous, and void of all reason"—clearly shows that Christianity is trying to absorb a belief here and to remove the pagan nature of a site, the reason why a chapel was built here.

In several cases, the spirit of the spring or fountain remains a dangerous, zoomorphic being to which the literature of the romances often lends the guise of a snake. In the *Lancelot-Grail,* we thus see Lancelot coming upon a clear spring welling up in the shadow of two sycamores. He drinks of its water and becomes ill, "his eyes rolled back in his head and he lay there senseless like a corpse." The people there saw "two enormous, long, hideous adders chasing one another. After a long pursuit, they reentered the spring, one after the other," from which the old woman accompanying the hero deduced that the spring's water was poisoned. A gentle maiden there gathered simples and made a potion from them that she administered to Lancelot.[11]

In the romance of *Perceforest* (early fourteenth century), the Venemous Fountain, whose bubbling water kills anyone who tastes it, plays a large role.[12] The queen of fairies placed a guard upon it to warn travelers and she predicted that Passelion *"would imprison the devil that poisons the water."* The anonymous author uses devil and evil spirit interchangeably. While Passelion is standing at the fountain's edge, a tempest carries him off to Norway, but his good spirit, Zephyr, teaches him *conjurations that are good against the devil,* then returns him to the fountain from which emerges a kind of "fish with a serpent's head, griffon's feet, and the tail of a scorpion, which was wondrously huge." The monster attacked Passelion, throwing him to the ground and seeking to drag him into the water, but the knight slew it:

> The evil spirit left the fish and went back into the fountain, then
> emerged again transformed into a bull.

Passelion killed the bull and forced the spirit to remove the poison from the fountain and then go away. The spirit dove back into the water, and a horrible din was created that lasted for a day. Passelion then realized that the *evil devils* had carried off a tree-covered mountain, and that the water of the fountain now formed a lake, "since named the *Estang Helain le Gros.*"

There is a monster in the twelfth-century Welsh romance of *Peredur ab Evrawc* (Peredur son of Efrawg) called the Addanc, which lives in a cave near a lake. Peredur comes to the castle of the King of the Tortures and helps in the resurrection of the dead recently slain by the Addanc. Every day the young men struggle in vain to kill the monster. Peredur is determined to aid them, but they refuse his help, for if any misfortune should befall him, it would be impossible to bring him back to life. Peredur sets off all the same and comes across a splendid woman sitting on top of a hill (an inhabitant of the other world, the *síd*), who gives him much information about the Addanc. She also gives him a stone that will make him invisible but still allow him to see the monster when he enters the grotto. Peredur slays the beast and beheads it. Etymologically, Addanc means "beaver," but here designates a water spirit that is obviously engaged in a mythical struggle with the knights of the King of the Tortures who, because their king owns a cauldron of resurrection, never die definitively. In the background a combat between supernatural beings for ownership of a domain can be glimpsed.

It is helpful here to also cite a passage from *Florimont* by Aymon de Varennes (late twelfth century) as it interestingly connects the theme of the spirit of the fountain with that of the founding of a city.[13] Philip, the ancestor of the Macedonians (not to be confused with the father of Alexander the Great), finds himself forced to fight a lion that has settled near a spring surrounded by a green prairie at the heart of a territory it has devastated completely. This animal's gaze has the singular feature that it drives anyone who looks at it mad. After a long battle, Philip slays the lion and founds the city of Pheliopolis on the devastated land, thereby reintegrating a new space into civilization with this gesture, which makes him a cultural hero.

In addition to the zoomorphic and sometimes undefined creatures that haunt the waters, we meet other mysterious figures. In *Li chevaliers as deus espees* (The Knight of the Two Swords), written after 1230, there is an intriguing motif that remains undeveloped: just what is this dwarf garbed in light spied by the story's hero, Meriadues, and who leads a multitude of beasts to drink at the fountain?[14] Is it the spirit of the spring or is it the spirit of the wood in which this water wells up? The romance of *Cristal et Clarie,*[15] written toward the end of the thirteenth century, presents an arm that haunts a fountain and drags off any individual that ventures too close to the water. This episode is reminiscent of a Grimm's fairy tale, *Iron John,* in which the arm belongs to a wild man, who is apparently amphibious as he lives at the bottom of a bog (he was uncovered when the pool was emptied), and who forbade any hunting in the forest. Any hunters who entered were never seen again. Incidentally, we may note the dual nature of this being, both spirit of the pool (marsh?) and of the forest, whose animals would be his herd. Furthermore, this figure is the master of a fountain that turns all that falls into it into gold.

Let us return to *Cristal et Clarie* and examine it more closely. Cristal comes upon an enclosed chapel. Near it flows a spring overshadowed by a tree. He goes toward it, thinking to quench his thirst, but a voice tells him not to. He looks up and sees a young girl, Lysarde, whom the devil of the fountain placed there because an evil fairy had, at her birth, predestined her to be given to the demon. In fact there are two demons: one is in the fountain, and his hand must be lopped off in order to defeat him (*trenchier la main de cel luiton / qui en le fontaine gist el boillon;* 6008–9); the other lives in the tree. When Cristal bends down, pretending to drink, the goblin's arm shoots out and, on the third attempt, the hero manages to chop it off; the goblin howls but remains invisible. Cristal next confronts the demon of the tree, a being that has two griffin heads, one at the regular place, the other in his chest. He kills it and makes his way into the chapel that houses the demon's treasure. This is in a wardrobe where a snake is coiled, guarding it. Cristal slays this serpent. Through the presence of the demons, the enchanted spot had become a *locus terribilis.* Probably expelled by the building of the chapel—which is synonymous with the Christianization of the site—the land spirit had managed to return in force and seems to have tripled itself.

Everything suggests that fairies were not the sole anthropomorphic manifestation of water spirits. Dragons and even dwarves could also claim this title, which provides ample evidence that is necessary for grasping and precisely assessing these traditions in which beliefs, myths, and literature are mingled. In Snorri Sturluson's *Prose Edda,* the dwarf Andvari can to a certain extent be considered the spirit for the waterfall that bears his name, Andvarafors. In fact, this is where he likes to frolic in the form of a pike. In my study of dwarves and elves I have shown that undeniable links existed between the figures called dwarves and the aquatic element, and moreover, this association turns up in medieval German literature.[16]

Let us now examine a more literary aspect that shows up primarily in the tales, and which provides evidence that a transformation of earlier beliefs went hand in hand with a certain rationalization of the fairy figures.

Certain fountains in the romances are apparently regarded as gates to the Other World and it seems that here we have a completely normal evolution of belief in land spirits. These spirits are often imagined to be like humans so not only are they attributed with human feelings but they are also given a habitat. If they live in a lake or spring, they must have a dwelling there, and it is in this way that the aquatic element, as in Frédéric de la Motte-Fouqué's *Undine,* becomes a kind of mist or fog that conceals a supernatural kingdom. In his *Liber de Nymphis, sylphis, pygmaeis et salamandris et de caeteris spiritibus* (Book of Nymphs, Sylphs, Pygmies, and Salamanders and Other Spirits), Paracelsus even claims in the context of his theory of elementary spirits, with respect to undines and water sprites, that water is their air and therefore they are unable to live outside this element. In the beginning of the thirteenth century, Gervase of Tilbury indicated that in a Gerona bishopric in Catalonia, there was a high mountain called Canagum (no doubt the Canigou) with a lake at its peak. "Found there, it is said, is a dwelling of demons as large as a palace with the door shut; but the dwelling and the demons remain unknown to the common folk" (*Otia Imperialia,* III, 66). The spirits of springs, lakes, and fountains became fairies who owned lands and castles in or under the lakes. The most famous of these fairies is certainly the Lady of the Lake who kidnapped and raised Lancelot in her kingdom hidden beneath an expanse of water.

Several romances thus provide episodes in which a knight vanishes inside a fountain. *Jaufré,* written around 1180, basically says the following:

> Jaufré heard a voice coming from a fountain. He hastened to the spot and found a lady drowning there while her companion was grieving at its edge. He tried to pull the lady from the water, but the other woman pushed him in and jumped in after, and the trio arrived in a paradisiacal Other World. The Fairy of Gibel, this was the lady's name, needed help to vanquish Felon d'Auberne, a giant devastating her lands.[17]

In Germany, the B version of *Wolfdietrich,* a long epic romance of the thirteenth century, presents Billunc, a wild man also called a "dwarf," who carries off the beautiful Liebgart, the widow of King Ortnit, to his castle located beyond a fountain that can only be traversed by carrying a certain plant in one's mouth (795ff). In *Demantin,* a romance written by Berthold von Holle in the thirteenth century, the knight Kamphyant is the husband of a fairy living in a lake. His helmet is adorned with stones allowing him to live underwater (verse 2400ff).

In the Celtic literature, the story titled *The Hunt of Slieve Guillean* tells how Finn was lured by a stag to a lake where he found a weeping maiden. She had lost her ring in the water. Finn dove in, recovered the ring, and returned as an old man who even his dogs failed to recognize.[18] It is obvious that he had been in contact with the Other World, for one characteristic of the latter is its possession of a time different from that of humans. This is evident through countless legends, such as that of King Herla, where three days spent in the kingdom of the dwarves was the equivalent of two hundred years, and in the legend of Guingamor, where three days in the kingdom of fairies corresponded, more logically, to three hundred years.

Another Celtic story, *The Pursuit of Gilla Decair and His Horse* (Tóruigheacht an Ghiolla Deacair agus a Chapaill), allows us to see how these themes are connected with one another:

> On a hill, Dermot discovered an island with a large tree covered with fruits and surrounded by a circle of stone pillars, a place whose sacred nature is indicated by this simple description. The largest overlooked a bubbling fountain with a drinking horn that Dermot used. A wizard champion emerged, reproached him for having drunk this water, and challenged him. The combat lasted until evening when the unknown adversary vanished into the fountain. Dermot slew two stags for food, the stranger reemerged, and during the ensuing battle both ended up entering the fountain and made their way to a magnificent country.[19]

What is interesting here is the motif of the object connected to the fountain that, above, indicates one cannot drink water from a spring with impunity without having been given permission by its owner, an action that prompts the appearance of a being from the Other World. In *Lanzelet,* which Ulrich von Zatzikhoven wrote around 1190 based on an unfortunately now lost French source text, Lanzelet makes his way to the heart of Behforet (Belle Forest) and finds a spring beneath a linden tree from which a mallet and a bronze cymbal are hanging. When the cymbal is struck three times, the lord of this site, Iweret (who happens to be a king of the Other World) emerges. It seems to me that this kind of story represents a literary treatment of a primitive outline: what is presented here as a provocation, or even a convocation, must have been a substitute for the motif of consciously or unconsciously offending the land spirit.

The episode of the Fountain of Barenton in Chrétien's *Yvain* reflects the same theme: pouring water on the sill of the fountain with the help of a goblet causes a devastating storm and the arrival of a knight, Escadoc the Red, who calls Calogrenant, and then Yvain, to account for allowing this sacrilegious action. Here again, the sequel to this action is the hero's entry into the Other World as he pursues the knight he has mortally wounded. The wondrous aspect is reduced and nearly erased here as it no longer necessary to dive into the water to reach the fairy kingdom. This reworking of the theme was probably due to the fact that the architecture of Barenton Fountain prohibits diving, and furthermore it falls under the category of the real since anyone can observe the actual existence of this fountain with their own eyes.

20
The Forest

Next to water, the forest is the great lair or refuge of land spirits. It is a haunted place, an outlying space full of violence; a site of exclusion; a refuge of outcasts and exiles as well as pagan beliefs; a place of marvels and perils; a savage, marginal, dreadful space; as well as a focal point of peasant memory. It is in the forest where we most often find those fountains and springs that were discussed in the previous chapter. The fairy Ninienne or Vivian loved to linger at the edge of the fountain of Briosques Forest, and Melusine and her sisters near the one in the forest of Coulombiers. Here roams the mythic wild boar, *li blans pors,* hunted by King Arthur's knights; here is where the Mesnie Hellquin travels as do the hosts of Diana and Herodiades.

A headquarters for strange phenomena that represent all sorts of theophanies, the forest is omnipresent in medieval literature. The *Lancelot-Grail* refers to the forest with evocative names such as the Adventurous, the Strange, the Lost, the Perilous, the Desvoiable (unmanageable), and the Misadventurous Forest. All the texts emphasize its disturbing nature with adjectives that recur repeatedly: *oscure* (obscure), *sostaine* (remote), *tenebreuse* (dark), *estrange* (strange), *salvage* (wild). Moreover, the forest is almost always long and wide (*longue, lee*) and extremely old (*des tens ancienor*). The romance of Claris et Laris says of one of them:

> *Too fierce and large is the forest*
> *and full of far too many great marvels. . . .* (3292)
> *The fairies have there their stage*
> *In one of the beautiful trees. . . .* (3317)

The Anglo-Norman poet Wace writes in the *Roman de Rou* of Brocéliande forest:

> *There is where the fairies come*
> *that the Bretons tell us can be seen*
> *as well as many other marvels.* (6387)

In short, the forest is a veritable conservatory of paganism and this is why a thousand supernatural creatures frolic here where they have found refuge after being driven from their territories by the advance of man. Moreover, throughout the Germanic realm, the forest often extends over the foothills of the mountains, thereby combining the mythical nature of both places.

The major problem encountered by the researcher is the following: to what extent are the dwarves, giants, dragons, and wild men found there the fictionalized vision of former land spirits? To answer this question, we must rely on the permanent features we have noted from other sites: a figure jealously keeping watch over his land and forbidding anyone from entering or killing game there, an individual (monstrous or not, or even replaced by a monster) demanding a tribute from his human neighbors, and a pronounced paganism.

In the thirteenth-century story *Virginal,* of which there are several extant versions, the lady bearing this name rules over a dwarf people in the wooded mountains of the Tyrol. She has a terrible neighbor, Orkîse, who demands a young girl from her as an annual tribute. Who is this figure whose name clearly indicates he is regarded as an ogre (*orco*)? He is probably the literary or legendary avatar of the spirit of these forests. I would like to point out that in a legend from the Berry region it is said that the young girls of Ennordes draw lots every year to determine which will go find the monster waiting for her in the middle of the forest. But rather than get caught up in a game of riddles with all the risks that entails, I would prefer to focus on three figures who maintain distinctive relationships with the sylvan environment: Merlin, Oberon, and Zephyr.

The son of a demon incubus, a devil given an angelic cast, and a protector of chivalry, Merlin is a complex and syncretic figure. Despite the many studies devoted to him, he remains a shadowy figure in various respects. From his father he inherited his abilities of being everywhere at once, metamorphosis, and knowledge of the past, but he received his gift of prophecy from God. According to the romance *Perlesvaus,* when Merlin died it was impossible to bury him in the chapel and his coffin was empty because his body disappeared when it was placed inside, carried away either by God or by the enemy. He was covered with hair at birth and once grown up he was large, strong, thin, brown, and hairy. Geoffrey of Monmouth depicts him as demented and living like a wild man who is constantly returning to the forests after being torn from their midst (*Vita Merlini;* 1–112). He shows him riding through the forest on a stag and leading a herd of bucks, deer, and wild goats (451ff), as he knows how to compel the obedience of animals like the churl in Chrétien's *Yvain.* In the *Vulgate Merlin,* he is called the "wild man" and uses this term when referring to himself. He also sometimes assumes the appearance of a white stag.[1] In *Le Livre d'Artus* (The Book of Arthur), Merlin appears as the master of the fountain of storms, he dwells in a hollow oak, and states: "I want you to know that my habit is such that I like to remain in the woods by the nature of the one who engendered me."[2] Geoffrey of Monmouth tells us that when King Aurele sent emissaries in search of Merlin, he was found in the corner of the mysterious forest near the fountain of Galabes, in the land of the Gewisséens. Robert de Boron's *Merlin* also emphasizes the close bond connecting him with the forest: *Je voil que vos sachiez qu'il me convient par fine force de nature estres par foies eschis de la gent.*[3]*

---

*I see you know that my nature compels me to keep a good distance from people.

Let us consider the features that allow us to see that the Merlin of the romances was undoubtedly once a forest spirit, an aspect that the authors largely concealed by making the seer the son of an incubus as a way to explain his powers. Merlin is the master of animals; he can take any form he pleases at will. Now we know that it is an identifying characteristic of spirits that they only take form to show themselves to humans. He has command over the elements and, most importantly, there is this one recurring motif: he cannot stay away for a long time from what we should consider his natural element. This detail inevitably brings to mind legends such as those of Melusine, in which the fairies who wed mortals must bathe once a week in total solitude, sometimes in the form of a serpent, which is the customary form of water spirits.

By means of the widespread belief in incubi from the twelfth century on, the figure of Merlin was integrated into the human universe and the world of the romances, and the only clues that still connect him to his true origin are those cited above. Edmond Faral cites a thirteenth-century poem, *Le Dit de Merlin Merlot* (The Tale of Merlin Merlot), which depicts Merlin as a kind of wood spirit, and remarks: "The woodland figure that appears here, so different from the type depicted by the French romances of the Arthurian cycle, perhaps answers to some ancient superstitions, independent of traditions that would be, strictly speaking, Breton."[4] Faral's intuition is remarkable because he did not have at his disposal the studies made since that show that two different figures were melded together to create the fictional character known throughout the world.

If we now turn our eyes to Oberon, who appears in *Huon de Bordeaux* (ca. 1220),[5] the deductions made about Merlin find confirmation because we again discover many elements in common. Oberon, depicted as a dwarf because his small size is due to the curse of a fairy at his birth, dwells in "a very vast and dreadful forest. . . . None who enter this wood can ever escape it if he speak to him, if he even spend but a moment in his presence he can never again leave the wood for the rest of his life." This amounts to imprisonment inside the Other World.

Oberon possesses great powers; when he is angry he causes wind and rain and can even break the trees. He is a master of spells and charms, and can even cause a wide river to appear. Furthermore, like any good fairyland being, he possesses magical objects and can go wherever he desires in the blink of an eye.

He is introduced as a Christian, but one detail shows that he belongs in fact to a pre-Christian past: he was born before Christ himself. He also knows the past and knows all about young Huon's life. While Merlin's powers are attributed to the singular manner of his conception, those of Oberon are the same as those held by fairies. We find ourselves in the same register in each but in the first case it is diabolical and in the second, simply wondrous.

One final detail of great importance for our study concerns the mastery of animals. "All the birds, beasts, or wild boars, wild and ferocious as they might be, come to me willingly once I beckon to them with my hand." In an earlier study of the superimposed strata found in this figure, I showed—fairly convincingly, I believe—that Oberon was an elf rather than a dwarf, but this does not exclude his being a woodland spirit because in the Middle Ages all these creatures were conflated, and their attributes and nature were blended together for literary needs.[6] In *Huon de Bordeaux* the spirit is interpreted and presented benevolently and becomes in some way Huon's guardian angel. However, his supernatural abilities, which essentially only manifest in the forest, are those of the land spirit.

With the romance of *Perceforest,* we see the appearance of another extraordinary character, Zephyr, who is depicted as a malicious and mischievous sprite. While Estonné is riding in the Selve Carbonnière, his horse comes to a sudden halt, and the demon possessing it, Zephyr, introduces himself as a fallen angel. He is a demon of fairly high rank in the hierarchy of spirits and has the gift of transforming himself at will. He says he does this to conceal his ugliness: "And when it pleases me, he transmutes another form to cover my ugliness when I wish to become familiar with a person" (II, 97v°).

He generally assumes the appearance of an old man clad in a home-spun cloak, which brings to mind the "hooded spirits" (*genii cucullati*). The substance of his body appears to be air, the gust of wind from which he takes his name: "You have no more power against my vengeance," he tells Estonné, "than you would have against a strong wind that hurled you into a ditch" (II, 96v°). Moreover, he goes wherever his whims lead him. He renders great service to his protégé and other knights, and, when the Romans sought to invade Great Britain, he tormented them and prevented them from disembarking, an action that likens him precisely to a genius loci, a *landvættr*.

The commonalities and differences between the three figures we have just met are quite revealing. All three have a supernatural origin—diabolical or fairylike. All like to live in the forests and come to lend assistance to those they have chosen; all have wondrous powers at their disposal, but it is in Merlin, "the savage," that the ancient, or more exactly pagan features are best preserved. Using the information collected, we can try to draw up a typology of the forest spirit, as it appears in the romances:

1. He is a marginal figure that can never remain long in the world of men.
2. He existed long before Christianity but has been integrated into the medieval Christian world by means of religious legends (the myth of fallen angels), scholarly and clerical beliefs (the generative power of incubi), and belief in the existence of fairies (the origin of Oberon, who according to some texts is the son of Julius Caesar and the fairy Morgue).
3. The beneficial actions of these figures contradict their origins and are a reflection of their integration into the courtly world, and of the manner in which they have been induced to conform to the civilization of a specific era. A kind of redemption for their original flaw can be seen in the cases of Merlin and Zephyr.

4. The forest spirit is a master of the animals and he also has power over the course of time in his domain.

5. He can take either animal or human shape.

In short, even when tamed he remains an ambiguous and disturbing being that retains a hint of deviltry: Zephyr loves to play tricks, Merlin loves to mystify those he serves, and Oberon is easily angered and will do his worst when thwarted unless one of his vassals is found to calm him down. Outside of their literary transformation, equivalent to that of all the fairies, these figures are evidence of the persistence of ancient beliefs, even if the romances have a tendency to make them a kind of literary *deus ex machina* or a burlesque element.

We may now take a look at the mountain, one of the high spots for beliefs and chivalrous adventure.

21
The Mountain and Its Spirits

Like the forest, the mountain is an amazing conservation area for paganism and its beliefs.[1] It should be recognized that it is the subject of countless myths. Quite often it is the cosmic mountain that connects the human world to that of the gods, revealing hell in its depths and heaven at its peak. It is the dwelling place for countless spirits that take the form of giants, dwarves, fairies, or monstrous animals. The mountain haunts the medieval imagination. Saint Augustine noted in his *City of God* (IV, 8) that the ridge of the mountains was under the protection of the goddess Collatina. Around 800, the anonymous text the *Reason to Catechize the Peasantry* forbid the consulting of auguries on the mountains (§81) and as early as the sixth century we come across a conjuration mixing paganism and Christianity for banishing spirits and demons in the forests, valleys, and mountains:

> In the name of our Lord Jesus Christ, I declare to you, unclean and diabolical spirit, that the angel Gabriel delivered from bonds of fire, you who beat ten thousand barbarous names. After the Lord's resurrection you came to Galilee. There He forbade you from taking possession of the wooded lands, the vales, and mountains so that you

could cause no harm to men . . . or cause hailstorms. Know then, most unclean diabolical spirit, that everywhere you can recognize the Scripture or hear the name of the Lord, you cannot harm as you please.[2]

This text confirms that demons lived in the places mentioned and allows us to interpret all these chapels and monasteries erected in the wild: once God's name was spoken in them, the demons were expelled from these spaces.

Gervase of Tilbury speaks of a boulder "whose side is pierced with windows as if it were a wall. To travelers far away, it looks like two or three women are there conversing . . . but when they draw near, the vision vanishes. . . . There is a huge boulder in Catalonia with a fairly extensive flat surface. On its summit around midday, knights in shining armor can be seen jousting. But if someone goes closer, none of that can be seen."[3] Even today, the names of some peaks in the Alps testify to their former inhabitants; Alpine and Pyrenean legends attest to them ad infinitum,[4] where this peak is nothing less than a petrified giant, that avalanche is the work of the land spirit, and the shepherds of the alpine summer meadows can all tell their own stories about encounters with the spirits.

In the medieval romances the mountain spirit essentially assumes three forms: that of a monstrous beast who has settled there, that of a giant, and that of a knight responsible for misrule. While the monstrous animal sometimes dwells in a cave, the giant and knight reside in a castle, a rude enclosure built of branches, or a fort, but we should be aware that in these cases we are dealing with a feudalized form of the original supernatural being.

The *Chanson des Chétifs*[5] tells how Baudoin de Beauvais confronted the monstrous dragon who had eaten his brother Hernoul in the cave where he lived (*en la roche cavee*) on Mount Tygris. No weapon could cut its hide, a demon inhabited its body (*diable avoit el cors*) and it wore a stone on its brow that gave off a great light:

El front ot perre qui luit et reflambie
Don't por nuit voit cler com por plaine midie*

This stone could be nothing other than a garnet. This is evident through a comparison of the above quote with a passage from *Gui de Warewic*:

[escaboucle] que la nuit jetout tele resplendeur,*
cum ço fust la clarté d'un jur.† (11033–34)

The garnet of the Mount Tygris monster makes our dragon similar to the wyverns that allegedly wear a stone like this at their brow. With the help of God, who uses Baudoin to perform a miracle, the reptile is vanquished and the demon departs in the form of a crow:

I. diaules li est parmi la gole issus . . .
en guise d'un corbel.‡

The demon then raises a terrible storm that is dissipated when the Abbot of Fescamp makes the gesture of benediction. The devil then dives into a nearby river and good weather returns.

Analyzing this text, Francis Dubost notes: "What we may be seeing here is a Christian adaptation of the archaic and aquatic component of the symbolism attached to the dragon."[6] Indeed, but there is more: the union between dragon or wyvern and demon; the devastation of the land, and the slaying of every man who risks a day and a half journey to Mount Tygris; the loosing of the tempest when the devil was expelled from the body to which it had given life—these are all clues that reveal the adaptation of an ancient model. The dragon is, in fact, the form of

---

*The stone on its forehead sparkled like flame / and its light made the night as clear as midday.
† [a garnet] that in the night cast such splendor, / that it was as light as day
‡ The devil, he was among the vermin that left . . . / in the guise of a crow.

the land spirit that is depicted as a devil. With the beast slain, the spirit abandons its outer form but remains on site, trying to drive away the humans by means of a storm. However, he has to leave the place once and for all when it has been blessed. The symbolism of Christianity's victory over paganism has been superimposed over that of man's victory over the land spirit. It is partially concealed but the result is the same: a new area has been colonized and civilized.

In *Le Roman d'Auberon* (The Story of Oberon),[7] written between 1260 and 1311, which in effect forms the prologue of *Huon de Bordeaux,* there is one episode that can be interpreted similarly, although it does not involve the devil. Oberon's brother George, who flees after abducting the sultan of Babylon's daughter, is resting with her on Mount Noiron, "a steeper mountain was never seen" (1854), near a spring. While he is sleeping an enormous snake approaches. His girlfriend awakens him and he battles the monster that spits fire and flame (1873); he slays it but he is grievously wounded. From the fictional perspective, what we have here is a marvelous episode emphasizing George's valor, but in the underlying archetypal thinking, we can make out one simple notion: every wild place is dangerous because it belongs to its first inhabitants, the land spirits.

It is indeed baffling to see that the mountain is also often the stage for battles between a thousand different unusual creatures. In *La Chanson d'Aspremont* (The Lay of Aspremont),[8] the Duke Naimes encounters this way a griffin, leopards, scorpions, crocodiles, and a mysterious *aufarïon* (1972) after having endured a terrible blizzard and barely escaping an avalanche of ice blocks detached by the wind. The mountain of Aspremont appears to be doing everything in its power to prevent Naimes from reaching the summit, as if the spirit of this place, under various animal shapes, was trying to forbid any violation of his domain.

In *La Mort Aymeri de Narbonne* (The Death of Aymeri of Narbonne),[9] there is a nine-headed wyvern that has settled on a mountain. It casts flames and cannot be enchanted (*enguigniée*), meaning that no means of magic can harm it. It has moved into the troglodyte castle of Roquebrune, which had been carved out of the rock by fairies in an earlier age. Guillaume made himself the champion of his people by succeeding to behead the monster that the storyteller converts into a devil (*aversier*). The place has therefore been purified and the archetypal power that ruled there eliminated, thus pacifying the region. This kind of combat strongly resembles an eviction.

In the romance of *Fergus*,[10] which dates from the first third of the thirteenth century and was written by William the Clerk of Normandy, only vestiges of this kind of legend remain. The Black Mountain is topped by a chapel defended by a hideous churl, but he is in bronze and cannot move. The path leading to the summit was carved by a giant of olden times "who dwelt in the forest" (2058). Francis Dubost is well justified in remarking that "the device of intimidation set up here was based on a simulacrum intended to reactivate certain fears . . . fed by the remnants of a forgotten belief, perhaps related to an ancient god of the mountain."[11] This notion about the reactivation of beliefs seems to me to be applicable to the works cited earlier.

In Great Britain, the twelfth-century Welsh romance of Peredur son of Efrawg offers a series of singular encounters, one of which corresponds perfectly with those we have just been examining. Peredur has vanquished the Black Opresser and asks him to tell him how he lost one eye. The other answers:

> I lost it in fighting the Black Serpent of the Carn. There is a mound, which is called the Mound of Mourning; and on the mound there is a carn, in the carn there is a serpent, and on the tail of the serpent there is a stone, and the virtues of the stone are such that whoever should hold it in one hand, in the other he will have as much gold as he may desire. And in fighting with this serpent was it that I lost my eye.[12]

The union of the wild place, the monster, and the wondrous stone clearly indicates that the serpent of the carn was, in the underlying mythical thought, something other than a simple reptile hiding in the rocks.

In the continental Germanic realm, it is especially in the stories surrounding Theoderic of Verona (Dietrich von Bern) that we find creatures appearing which must have originally been land spirits.[13] In these legendary poems, whose plot most often takes place in the Tyrolean mountains, we essentially see dwarves, giants, and dragons. All epic exaggeration and fabulation aside, on every occasion that one of these creatures appears it tries to prohibit entry into the wild places.

Deviltry is never the culprit; it is always the hostile, trackless space of a closed world abounding in unusual creatures: centaurs, wild maidens, the three queens of Jochgrimm from *Das Eckenlied,* a populace of dwarves governed by Laurin who also knows how to compel the obedience of the giants (*Laurin, Walberan*), countless dragons (*Dietrichs erste Ausfahrt*), a cursed hunter (*Wunderer*), and an ogre (*Virginal*). Even when taking clichés into account, significant facts remain such as those giants that are so savage they live apart from their fellow giants and are practically ferocious animals in terms of both clothing and appearance, and in how they react toward a man's approach. They will attack him by uprooting a tree if their club is not at hand. They defend their territory and their game (see part 2), or demand a tribute from the traveler, which may be his left foot and his right hand—the left foot because that is the one used to mount a horse, and the right hand because it is used to wield a sword. In other words, the knight is rendered helpless and condemned to certain death.

The simultaneous emergence of two beings—a monstrous man and a beast, or often a giant and a dragon—raises an extremely interesting problem that we shall tackle next.

22

The Problem of
Parédrie

Based on a considerable body of work, Henri Dontenville advanced the hypothesis, later echoed by Francis Dubost, that a "bond of *parédrie*" existed, *in illo tempore,* between the monsters guarding a wild space under a dual form, human and animal.[1] *Parédrie* refers to a relationship of two supernatural beings to one another, with the one accompanying or literally "sitting beside" the other (the term derives from Greek *para*, "next to, by," and *édra,* "seat"). The accompanying spirit or creature can be termed a paredrus. In medieval literary works, a paredrus in human form would be a means of integrating the monster into the feudal world by using the narrative frameworks that were appropriate to the day and age. With the support of various texts we have been considering, this hypothesis can be transformed into a certainty.

In *Florimont,* for example, the author Aymon de Varennes introduced the wyvern and the giant Garganeüs at the same time, as if they were one and the same entity (1963ff). Both threatened the same country and demanded a tribute consisting of people and animals. This tribute must be regarded as the sacrifice necessary to obtain the spirits' relative neutrality. In *The Golden Legend* by Jacobus de Voragine, the dragon slain by Saint George lived in an immense lake, and the inhabitants of Silcha first brought it two sheep a day and later, when sheep became scarce, one sheep and a man. Moreover, Garganeüs could not be killed except by the sword that the fairy of Isle Celée gave to Florimont. These elements can be better understood if we compare them to the late fifteenth- or early sixteenth-century work titled *Das Lied vom Hürnen Seyfrid* (The Lay of Horn-Skinned Seyfried).[2]

In this medieval Low German text, a flying dragon abducts the beautiful Kriemhild and carries her off to a high mountain. This dragon is in fact a transformed man accompanied by a devil. When Seyfried (= Siegfried) reaches the mountain, he runs into the giant Kuperan who functions as the guardian of the mountain. He alone knows where the door is (strophe 86), for which he holds the key (strophe 99), and he knows the location of the sword that alone can slay the beast (strophe 107). He does everything he can to prevent Seyfried from reaching the mountain but is killed after committing a triple betrayal (strophe 114). The hero casts him down to the foot of the mountain where he is crushed. The dragon's days are ended in much the same way. Seyfried cuts him in half with the sword and throws the pieces to the base of the mountain (strophe 148). What is most interesting is the set of motifs that make up this episode. Some light can be shed on them if we look at Lithuanian legends based precisely on a manifestation of the *parédrie* relationship. In these legends, the life of the dragon is entrusted to a third party, and the hero must take possession of it in order to kill the beast.

One hero orders the maid kidnapped by the dragon to inquire with cunning of the dragon: "Go and ask the gentleman where his *sveikata* [health] is."

The dragon gives himself away: "My *sveikata:* in the ninth kingdom lives my brother; if someone should slay him, then I too would not have my health."

The hero, of course, slays the dragon-brother from whose insides there falls an egg with which the first dragon is "destroyed." . . .

Another dragon, when asked, "Where is your *gyvastis* [life] since you are so strong that no one can kill you?" answers, "My *gyvastis* is far and deep: in the sea on an island there is a bull, in the bull, a dove, and in that dove, an egg, and in the egg—my *gyvastis*."[3]

In the feudal world, the myth that we find in the Lithuanian legends has been adapted and transformed into literature. It is a unique weapon of supernatural origin that plays the role of life, the *sveikatas* and *gyvastis* of the stories above. In every case, the dragon is depicted with starkly human features—he talks—and he is diabolical, which puts it in conformance with the civilization that gives the narrative its context.* In *The Lay of Horn-Skinned Seyfried,* the giant Kuperan is comparable to the dragon's brother that is guardian of his life, which clearly shows that an undeniable mythical relationship existed between the two beings, even if it was not perceived by the writer who reproduced archetypal patterns even though their meaning had been lost.

We can deduce a typology of the facts to show how the data is organized:

In a wild place two monsters—one human-like, the other animal-like—rule as masters; this is the fragmented and literatized form of the land spirit.

Both are devastating a land and are in open battle against men who can only appease their wrath through sacrifices.

They have been quite broadly demonized.

They are joined by a tenuous but solid bond, as the one we could call the main monster can only be slain once his *paredrus* has been killed.

The main monster can only be slain by a single weapon, the

---

*For example, in *Fouke Fitz Warin,* the dragon that Fouke confronts abducted a duke's daughter and brought her to a mountain where it forced her to wash its beard, face, and chest whenever it returned from a raid on which it had devoured some living being. This dragon, says the text, "was rational like a man."

possession of which the hero gained through various means (for example: a supernatural being gave it to him, he stole or extorted it from the double of the land spirit [a giant], and so forth).

It is probably worth looking at how the writers of the Middle Ages reused this kind of outline in a totally different context.

In his *Roman de Mélusine,* Coudrette tells how Pressine punished her three daughters, Mélusine, Melior, and Palestine. Mélusine was condemned to be a serpent every Saturday. Melior was charged with guarding a sparrowhawk in an Armenian castle, and Palestine with watching over the treasure of her father Helinas on Mount Canigou in Aragon. It should be noted that each of the sisters is associated with an animal and attached to a site enshrouded with legends.

In the case of Mélusine, a taboo had to be respected; in the cases of Melior and Palestine, an ordeal had to be overcome: it is necessary to

The lady of the castle of the Isle of Kos.
Illustration from The Travels of Sir John Mandeville.
Basel: Bernhard Richel, 1480–1481.

watch over the sparrowhawk for three successive nights without falling asleep. Whoever succumbs to sleep shall disappear; whoever attempts to steal the treasure of Helinas must confront monsters that act as guardians of the mountain and only allow the chosen ones to pass—in this case, a member of the family of Lusignan. Melior and Palestine therefore perform the duty of a land spirit, although this feature is more pronounced with Palestine's connection to monsters (reptiles, bears, and dragons) and the fact she is never seen, whereas the adventure of the sparrowhawk is entirely assimilated into the courtly universe. But in both cases, the ancient mythical outline has undergone considerable loss of meaning, which goes hand in hand with its aesthetic fictionalization, and it is transformed into a chivalrous ordeal.

23
A Composite Site
The Dwelling of Grendel and His Mother

We have seen that it is sometimes difficult to assign a being to a place because the site was often of a composite nature, uniting water and forest, forest and mountain, and sometimes all three elements of the landscape. A relative uncertainty prevails in some cases, which we will now examine.

This amalgam of geographical elements is best exemplified in the Old English poem *Beowulf,* the only extant manuscript of which dates from the late tenth or early eleventh century.[1] The tale itself creates a fantastical landscape that would be right at home in contemporary cinema. The poem devotes so much space to the descriptive elements of the domain ruled by the two monsters, Grendel and his mother, it is obvious a close bond joins them together. Let us take a look at the facts.

A large portion of this poem recounts Beowulf's struggle against Grendel and his mother, who every night attack the palace of King Hrothgar and make off with his warriors who they kill and devour. Grendel is demonized to the fullest possible extent. He is an "evil doer and a demon from hell" (*fyrene fremman feond on helle,* 101),

163

an "unholy wight" (*wiht unhælo,* 120), the "malevolent enemy of the human race" (712), a "heathen" (*hæþen,* 986), an "ill-famed creature" (762), and a "giant" (*eoten,* 761 and 1353). He is a "notorious stalker of boundaries who reigns over wasteland, fen, and moor" (verse 103). His father is unknown, "born before him among the dark spirits" (verse 1355–56). For twelve years, which can simply mean a very long time, he has devoured Hrothgar's warriors (147) and made his palace become gradually deserted (145–46).

His mother is a "vengeful creature" (1256), a "monstrous female" (*aglæcwif,* 1259), condemned to "dwell in awful waters, in icy currents" (1260–61). No weapon can cut her flesh nor that of her son (801–5). Both live in the "lake of monsters" (*nicera mere,* 845) and:

> . . . *They haunt a land*
> *of wild wolfslopes, wind-scourged headlands,*
> *fearsome fentracks. There a foaming stream*
> *down drops away past darkening cliffs—*
> *the flood flows beneath. Yet not far away*
> *by the mile-measure the mere stretches.*
> *Hoarfrosted heights hang above it,*
> *shrubs fast rooted shade the water.*
> *In the dusk glimmers a devilish marvel:*
> *flame on the flood. No freeman living,*
> *although old and wise, knows the unplumbed depths.*
> *. . . Not a pleasant place!*
> *Tumult of waters towers spuming*
> *to the scowling sky; scud, blown by winds,*
> *darkens the daylight, until dismal the gloom,*
> *the heavens weeping.* (1357–76)[2]

Like a ceaselessly recurring leitmotif, we find notions of darkness—Grendel "comes from the moor, below misty cliffs" (710); the moor is "murky" (1405)—along with desolation and wilderness: "steep, rocky cliffs, constricted tracks, a narrow single path, unknown route, past holes full of water-demons" (1409–10). When Beowulf nears the lake, the poem tells us that "suddenly he saw the cliff trees sloping above the slate-grey boulder, the woeful woodlands. Water lay below, bloody and turbid" (1414–16).[3] This was the habitat of "wights from elsewhere" (1500) and of creatures "mighty in malevolence" (verse 1339). This wild landscape is that of a yet uncivilized space and thus one that belongs, in the minds of the men of yesteryear, to the local land spirits, who were simultaneously devils, giants, and animals that could not tolerate humans living too closely to them. The situation is exactly the same when a dreadful dragon threatens a town and demands a daily or annual sacrifice, as in the legend of Saint George or that of the Graouilly of Metz.

It is the combination of a number of motifs—wild habitat, cannibalism, invulnerability, a quasi-amphibious nature, and the systematic attack of any humans that come too close to their lair—that permit us to classify Grendel and his mother as genii loci. One additional detail supports this deduction: Hrothgar and his people have called upon their gods to rid them of these monsters, but their prayers have been in vain (175–80). This means two things, depending on the perspective that is taken. From the Christian perspective, the gods are powerless because only the true God is humanity's best recourse. From the perspective of the pre-Christian mindset, the monsters and the gods are on the same plane with respect to their powers and their nature. Why would the gods intervene against their peers who live on earth and not in some far-off Valhalla?

Moreover, Beowulf again shows the survival of a mythical paredrus (Grendel and his mother). As we saw in the preceding chapter, this is a detail that gradually emerges as one of the fundamental elements for identifying land spirits beneath the disguises given them by epic or Christian romances. Furthermore, we again find an important detail that was noted above with regard to *The Lay of Horn-Skinned Seyfried*. The two monsters cannot be slain by a normal weapon, not even a sword forged by Wayland!* Grendel dies of the wound inflicted on him by Beowulf—he tore off his arm. Grendel's mother is slain by a blow from the sword the hero found in the underwater cave. It so happens that this is a supernatural weapon and the "work of giants" (1557–1563). It was inaccessible because it was in the cave at the bottom of the lake. One final detail: the elimination of the monsters allows humans to live in peace and prosperity.

The interpretation I propose here does not contradict the one I put forth in 1986, in which I demonstrated that behind the story of Grendel and his mother lay a tale about Germanic revenants. The current interpretation completes the former one, in fact, since any dead individual can turn into a local spirit and a great confusion reigned in the medieval mind between all these creatures whose boundaries were constantly shifting.[4] I will reiterate: the form of the incarnations of the "spirits" is irrelevant, all that matters is the action, its context, and the results of the elimination of the supernatural power that is hindering the happy outcome of human affairs. In particular, we must avoid conflating the literary and mythical planes, the fictional adaptation and the archetypal thought. Wild men, giants, dwarves, dragons, or other monsters, the dead finally, can all represent ad hoc incarnations of *numens,* but only when we find a set of converging motifs of the sort presented above. In the other cases, the battle against these creatures should be seen as a chivalrous adventure or a fairy tale, but one that implicitly conveys, in one way or another, the notion of the hero's initiation and inauguration.

Finally, we should note that swamps are, in the romances and later folk traditions, the stage for strange manifestations. They provide the borderland for the dwellings of unclassifiable figures like those of the house of garnets in Conrad von Stoffeln's *Gauriel von Muntabel* (3494ff);[5] and of the enchanter Malduk in Ulrich von Zatzikhoven's *Lanzelet;* and of Roaz de Glois in Wirnt von Grafenberg's *Wigalois.*

---

*[Wayland the Smith is the legendary weapon-maker who forges the magical sword for Siegfried in Germanic legends. —*Trans.*]

These places seem to be alive, as in Ulrich Füetrer's *Persibein,* in which a fantastic scene of disenchantment takes place (219ff). When Persibein reaches the Wild Swamp, whose howl can slay all living things, the ground shakes and trembles, and a thick cloud covers the sun. Thunder and lightning accompany echoing howls "as if the earth had swallowed hillocks and boulders," and a monstrous serpent appeared, spitting fire and stench. A tablet fell from its ear, on which it was written that he had to plunge his hand into the reptile's mouth and pull out whatever he found there. Persibein heeded this instruction, pulled out a toad, which he killed, and the monster turned into a beautiful young woman who died on the spot.

In the next chapter, we will take a more detailed look specifically at the role of the moor.

24

The Moor

We have just seen that in the composite landscape of Beowulf the moor is undoubtedly the principal place and it is, at any rate, the location where the other elements (stones, mountain, lake, and so on) were set. Like all wild spaces, the moor is disturbing and sometimes compared to a wilderness. In fact, in medieval Western thought, it truly is a wilderness. Fairies can be encountered there, as in *Le lai de Désiré* (The Lay of Désiré), or else it is a no man's land separating the land of men from that of fairies, as in *Seyfried von Ardemont* by Albrecht von Scharfenberg (both thirteenth-century works).

The romance of *Fouke Fitz Warin* includes a narrative sequence of the utmost value for our study of creatures who love nothing so much as shadow and mystery.[1] William the Bastard comes to the country of Wales, discovers a desolate burned town (*ars e gatee*), and learns:

> The castle was once called Chastel Brian, but its name now is Old March. Brutus, a very valiant knight, once came to this land with Corineus, from which Cornwall takes its name. . . . None lived here except so extremely ugly folk, huge giants whose king was named Goemagog. Hearing of Corineus's arrival, they set off to oppose him, but they were finally all slain except Goemagog, who was of wondrous size.

Brutus managed to drive the giant into the sea, where he drowned.

A devil spirit then entered Goemagog's body and defended this country for so long a time that no Briton dared live there. Much later, King Bran, son of Donwal, had the city rebuilt, the walls raised again, and the large moats fortified. . . . The devil came at night, took it away, and since then no one has lived there.

One of William's vassals, Payn Peverel, decides to tempt fate and spend the night in the ruins.

When night fell, the weather became so ugly, dark, and dim, accompanied by a storm of thunder and lightning, that all those there were so scared they could no longer move their hands or feet. They fell on the ground as if dead.

Payn Peverel then makes a prayer to heaven. Hardly has he finished when the devil appearing as Goemagog bursts out holding a club and spitting smoke and flames from his mouth. Peyn prevails over him and asks him what he is doing in this place, and he learns this:

When Goemagog died and gave his soul unto Belzebuth . . . , he entered his body and under his appearance came to this place to guard the huge treasure amassed by Goemagog and placed in a dwelling dug out beneath the ground of this town.

The treasure consisted of oxen, cattle, swans, peacocks, horses, and other animals cast in very fine gold. Twice a year the giants had the custom of honoring their god, the bull. Before this whole country was called the White Moor (la Blanche Lande), he and his companions enclosed the moor with high walls and deep moats. Since that time, the town had been filled with evil spirits who lured knights to jousts and tourneys on the moors from which they never returned. But Augustine, a disciple of Jesus, came to this spot and erected a chapel that much irked the spirits. After he predicted the future to Payn, the spirit abandoned Goemagog's body. The night grew brighter and the weather turned nice.

We find all the usual ingredients of Christianization in connection with the remnants of the more ancient past in this story. The first inhabitants of the country were giants, who were then replaced by evil spirits, namely by possessing the body of one of these monstrous men. These giants were pagans who worshipped idols. Bran colonized the site, but the spirits were stronger and drove him out and reoccupied the entire area, including the White Land. They made it an enclosed space, and therefore a sacred space, in which they imposed their law. The danger of the place is indicated by the chapel built by Augustine, which represents a kind of boundary marker, a border that Christians should not cross. This interpretation is strengthened by the first name of the area, the Old March; in other words, the former frontier between men and spirits.

One final detail shows that the devil possessing Goemagog's bodily form is in fact a spirit, a *daimon*. His appearance is connected with a change in the weather to a terrible storm. We have already seen a similar atmospheric phenomenon take place when a hero confronts a local spirit. This was the case in *La Chanson des Chétifs,* for example. Furthermore, Payn Peverel's victory is that of a cultural hero who eliminates the law that has reigned in this place since the beginning, expands the civilized space, and banishes a spirit that threatens all humans coming near its territory.

We always encounter the same mythic outline, the constancy of which is revealing and is necessarily based on the beliefs presented in the first part of this study. But we should not make the assumption that just anyone can get the best of a local land spirit, as we are going to see next.

25

The Hybridization of Myths

Readers will surely have noted that the vanquishers of local spirits are holy men or believers, which is one way of bringing the confrontation into the Christian sphere. Nevertheless, we ought to move beyond the level of simple observation and ask ourselves if something might be hidden beneath the obvious here.

In *Wigalois,*[1] which Wirnt von Grafenberg wrote at the very beginning of the thirteenth century, we meet the dragon Phetan who has devastated the land of Korentin:

> Roaz de Glois slew King Lar, and having formed an alliance with the devil, stole his lands. Larie, Lar's daughter, pled for aid at the court of King Arthur, and Wigalois offered to restore her lands to her. After various adventures, he learned that he had to slay the dragon that had appeared a dozen years before Lar's death, and which Roaz was unable to kill. In the form of a stag, the deceased Lar lured the hero to an isolated spot, reassumed human shape, and gave him a spear, the only weapon capable of killing the dragon. Wigalois successfully completed his adventure; killed Roaz in single combat after he got rid of Karrioz, a wild man or dwarf who had no marrow in

his bones; and traveled through a marsh covered in a black and petrifying fog. He married Larie and became lord of Korentin.

Behind these wondrous facts, athough simple in appearance, a double myth can be discerned. On the one hand, we have the return in strength of the spirit who until this point had been held in check by Lar's Christianity. On the other hand, there is that of a country's prosperity linked to the person of the legitimate sovereign.

King Lar puts his trust in Roaz, a pagan whose earldom borders Korentin, which is obviously a transgression and sin (4835ff), because he must spend ten years in Purgatory (verse 4819ff). Although the text never says so explicitly, it seems that Phatan appeared at the moment Lar formed a bond with Roaz. The dragon continuously devastates the land, which brings to mind both the dragon of Saint Marcellus and the one in *Beowulf,* whose appearance is triggered by a sin and a sacrilege. Phetan killed men and horses, and extended his activity everywhere except for the Wild March (*daz wilde mos,* 4692ff), territory in whose center stood the castle of Roaz, the pagan supported by the devil. Everything transpires as if Lar's transgression allowed the original powers, given concrete form by the dragon, to regain possession of this region. Now Lar was unable to defeat the dragon, which the usurper Roaz was also incapable of slaying.

On a mythic level this can be read as follows: because of his sin, Lar was no longer capable of fulfilling his duties as sovereign, and we know through extremely old myths that survive (among other things) in the Arthurian romances, that the person of the king is the guarantor for the land's prosperity. An ill king makes his land sterile, a sinful king will see his country destroyed.* Roaz's inability to level the monster confirms the likeliness of this interpretation: as an illegitimate sovereign this pagan had no power over natural forces.

---

*Compare the story of the *méhaigné* (wounded) king in the *Story of the Grail,* and the prehistory of the blow he received, which is related in the tale of Baalain (Balen).

We should in fact recall that in the Indo-European ideology of the three functions (first: royalty, priesthood; second: war; third: fertility, prosperity), the legitimate sovereign realizes the union of the three functions in his person. The first function presumes the recognition of the gods or spirits (*numens* or land spirits), which confers legitimacy. Roaz should be able to easily slay the dragon as he has made a pact with the devil, but the devil can obviously offer him no assistance in this instance. This is not a case of simple Christianization, but the repeating of a framework based on a myth of sovereignty and belief in land spirits.

Wigalois is depicted here as one of the chosen: "Now God has sent you here," Lar says, "so that you can free us. At the same time you will receive a reward that will gladden your heart forever; you shall have [the hand of] my daughter, Larie, as well as this land of Korentin" (4701ff). The hero therefore embodies the *miles christianus,* which is shown by another detail in the text: the spear that Lar gives him was brought by an angel (4748ff). It is the only thing that can kill Phetan: "No other iron forged exists that can cut the dragon, save for this unique spear," Lars tells him (4771ff).

Designated this way as the legitimate successor and given the support of the supernatural powers, Wigalois slays the dragon, and following a series of other adventures, manages to reintegrate Kornetin back into the feudal world. This judiciously Christianized story thereby conceals older beliefs and deceives the reader who has no points of comparison and consequently sees this as nothing other than a courtly adventure. This is probably how a thirteenth-century audience hearing this romance received it as well, because in all likelihood they no longer grasped the mythical framework that had been reconstituted for literary purposes and which resided in the collective unconscious.

The closer we come to the end of the Middle Ages, the more muddled the tracks become. Authors mixed themes and motifs, which had practically lost any connection to earlier myths, and fabricated a stereotypical world of marvels that strained all credibility, precisely because it superimposed too many elements from too many different sources. I believe Ulrich Füetrer (who died at the end of the fifteenth century) provides one of the best examples of this development. His Arthurian romances recycle various clichés within a completely misunderstood mythical structure. In *Persibein,* the following story is told in Adventures 31–32. I summarize it as follows:

While Persibein was staying at King Arthur's court, Kurie (a counterpart of Cundrie the Witch in *Perceval*) came in search of him because a demon (*wiht;* 486, 1) had kidnapped her son and Engiselor, a fairy. It had imprisoned the fairy on a high mountain and stolen her land, which was surrounded by a river (or sea, *wag*) that prevented anyone from entering or leaving it. Led by Kurie, who knew all the paths, Persibein made his way to the mountain, which was defended by a sea monster, Garmaneys (489, 5). This monster had to be defeated and then forced to take him to the top of the mountain, for there was no other way to the summit. Persibein succeeded in freeing Engiselor from her magically forged chains and also gained possession of magic stones that gave their bearer protection against fire and water. They also possessed other virtues that are not described.

The hero then makes his way to the island where the demon abductor, Wagollt, lives. He is able to cross over the water thanks to the wondrous stones and then sees a forest in flames (497), but this is only a magic illusion. Terrified when he sees nothing can stop Persibein, Wagollt refuses to fight the hero but instead offers him shelter. He steals his sword during the night as he intends to treacherously murder him. Engiselor learns of this thanks to her magic powers and comes to Persibein to give him armor. Walgollt and his men attack the valiant knight, who kills them all and frees many knights and ladies that this demon had imprisoned (510).

The events unfurl like a typical adventure and we can easily discern earlier models behind each motif. However, what we find here in an extremely stereotyped and literary form is a rich mythic substratum that combines two different structures. In fact, the plot unfolds on two planes (the mountain and the island) and features two victims (Engiselor and Kurie's son) and two antagonists (Wagollt and Garmaneys). Here we find a vestige of the mythic paredrus that we looked at earlier. In both cases the action takes place on a site that cannot be accessed by normal means and is protected by a guardian. The first confrontation is intended to provide Persibein the means of entering Wagollt's domain. If we refer to the outline of *The Lay of Horn-Skinned Seyfried,* we can glimpse the underlying mythic framework. This first action no longer provides Persibein with the weapon needed to slay his antagonist, but rather the means to get to him. This first movement is also comparable to Wigalois's meeting with King Lar, when the chivalrous knight receives the spear that will let him kill Phetan. The fact that the site is split in two, combined with Engiselor's presence, obscures the mythic substratum. This substratum can be summed up as follows:

> On a mountain, on an island, lives a demon that captures humans. Its lair is defended by a monster (Garmaneys) whose defeat is necessary for procuring an object or objects needed to defeat the demon.

By introducing the character of the fairy Engiselor, Ulrich Füetre conceals this framework and splits another motif in two. Engiselor brings Persibein a cuirass, and it is thanks to this armor that he is able to resist the attack of Wagollt and his men. Contrary to earlier traditions, the object is no longer one to be used offensively (sword, spear) but defensively. Nonetheless it comes from a supernatural being.

One final point is worth noting. The places are quite profoundly marked as sites of the Other World. When he is at the top of the mountain, Persibein has the impression of being in paradise (490, 4). He finds there a bright gold palace embedded with precious stones. Wagollt's castle is on an island and surrounded by a forest, which makes it a sacred space and a sanctuary, although here it is presented as simply the home of the demon. The demon's name, however, is quite revealing. Wagollt is a combination of *wag,* "sea," and the verb *walten,* "to rule," so the name has the meaning "Master of the Waters." He is therefore a merman—something we might have guessed since Garmaneys is described as a sea monster.

26

The Return of the Place Spirits

A successful colonization depends on conciliating the spirit of the place. The following chronology in a certain number of stories has probably caught the reader's attention: humans settle a piece of land while its spirit survives nearby, known or unknown to the settlers, and then the supernatural being returns in force. This is the case in *Fouke Fitz Warin* and in *Cristal et Clarie.* In *La mort Aymeri de Narbonne,* the spirit recaptures the underground castle built by fairies. In the Arthurian romances, we often find abandoned chapels that are home to strange manifestations and cemeteries haunted by demons. This is quite odd, as in both cases consecrated places are involved. How should we interpret these facts?

It would seem that land spirits are never vanquished once and for all. They can be repelled, but they remain vigilant, ever ready to seize any opportunity to take back their property. We should compare what hagiographic legends relate in this regard and what is said by epics and romances. In the hagiographies, the saints rarely kill the dragons and other zoomorphic manifestations of spirits, whereas in narrative literature the knights attack them violently and slay them. This difference is probably a normal result of the duties of the protagonists: a warrior is expected to use a sword and spear, and a saint to use religion. The spiritual arm is often more effective, especially when the adversary is a supernatural being. Accordingly, there is also a shift in perspective: the action takes place on a vertical plane (the axis of earth and heaven) instead of a horizontal one that is entirely of the earth.

It is worth lingering over a second point. What is it that allows the spirit to return or appear again? Many texts suggest one answer: it is a transgression (as in the story of Lar in *Wigalois,* or that of the theft of the cup in *Beowulf*) or a sin (as in the story of Saint Marcellus's dragon) or else the paganism of a site's inhabitants (as in the legend of Saint Taurin). In this Christian context, the moral lesson and the didactic intent are crystal clear. The monster that appears is a punishment, a sign of divine wrath, for as everyone knew in the Middle Ages, spirits, whatever form they took, could only cause harm to humans with God's permission.

But what is at work in the case of abandoned chapels that still offer material expression of the Christianization of a dangerous or pagan space? Christianity's sacred force never seems to be definitive and needs constant renewal. If no worship is performed in a chapel, its sacredness fades away and the eternal lamp no longer burns there. God is therefore absent and paganism can then reassert itself and those beings that Christianity had banished can return in strength. Chapels, monasteries, and hermitages are all centers of Christianized space, but they are isolated enclaves and small islands in a hostile territory—refuges for the knights wandering through savage lands. But there are also two forms of sacred power that exist in opposition among pagans, as we have seen. This conclusion must therefore be a nuanced one, as the problem of the regulation of the primordial sacred goes beyond the pagan/Christian split, and in fact predated it considerably.

The crosses we find erected at crossroads, on mountaintops, or in the villages (mission crosses) have a dual significance. They give material expression to the spiritual appropriation of the space and the establishment of the faith, but they also function like amulets or phylacteries intended to prevent the return of the pagan forces that once ruled here.

All those Christian monuments in the middle of nowhere also make it possible to find the ancient pagan centers—the places where the tutelary deities, who are often but one form of local land spirits, were worshipped. Look at all these chapels built next to springs or on hilltops, nearby or upon bridges, not to mention the niches in old houses that snugly hold a statue of the Virgin or a saint. These statues replaced the objects pagans used for protection, such as a horseshoe or owl nailed on the stable door (Alps) or carved horse heads adorning the ridge of the roof (Lower Saxony). In the more recent traditions, it is often hard to know just what one is seeking protection from, since all the beings of the night are gathered together under the evocative but vague term "spirit."

Afterword

Over the course of a difficult investigation—for the spirits are quite averse to being flushed from hiding—I have tried to show what lies hidden behind certain situations found in romances, epics, and legends. Various criteria for the recognition and identification of land spirits have been gradually brought into the open, which should allow for a more critical reexamination of medieval literature and a better perception of everything—including the traces of bygone mindsets and beliefs—that it transports like the flotsam and jetsam of a remote past.

Paganism and folk beliefs have certainly been presented in a veiled way. Initially, they were concealed by Christianization, and later by the literary treatment of the old facts of a remote past. Narrative literature "civilized" the spirits and transported them into the sphere of feudal civilization as giants, dwarves, elves, undines, dragons, and even birds, as well as strange knights imposing "male customs," and, finally, fairies. Hagiographical literature turned them into devils, and as it left its mark and vision of things on the educated class, the devil is everywhere. Up to this point, the great majority of studies have remained on the surface of things and taken their Christian interpretation of the data as fact, not taking into account that "devil" has a formidable polysemy, which makes it a cover name, a catch-all term that covers all the supernatural beings of paganism: gods, spirits, genies.

In order to write a history of land spirits, it was necessary to go beyond what the clerics and writers of the Middle Ages said, to read the earlier significance of the facts beneath the message they imposed, and to refuse to see only marvels in unusual accounts. It cannot be overstated that the marvelous is the fruit of the real—it is a Weltanschauung based on the structures of the imaginal realm, in which we quite often find the degraded forms of ancient beliefs whose shape may have changed but not their content.

Medieval literature represents an eclipse of sorts in the very long history of land spirits. From the sixteenth century on, they gradually shed their Christian and fictional veneer and once more showed their true face in the folk traditions that have been collected from that time up to the present day. For certain, their demonization tenaciously persists, today as in the past, but the spirits remain a formidable presence. They are little inclined to tolerate the sudden incursion of human beings into their territory. Humanity has banished them to increasingly remote regions with a battery of crosses, and the sound of church bells sends them fleeing. Nevertheless, the spirits are, and continue to be, inexorably connected to the sites—the maps prove it—and all attempts to eliminate them have been, at best, partial setbacks. The studies done by folklorists leave no doubt in this regard.

Mentalities are extremely slow to evolve, especially in rural areas, and the best examples are the extraordinary preserves of ancient traditions and legends such as the Alps and Pyrenees. Anyone who hikes along the back roads and footpaths will quickly discover the presence of spirits. Those two rocky peaks overlooking the Brenner Pass are the petrified forms of the giant Serles and his wife. Shepherds ever run the risk of encountering the Fangas or the Norgas, the Percht and the Saligen (benevolent fairies), who will either protect or exterminate their flocks. Voices rise from the mountain streams and waters, and when the dragon in the lake turns over or shakes his tail, it causes flooding. The Stumpfal, a cross erected on Mount Horn (Issime, Aosta Valley), prevents an evil spirit from sending hailstorms; the mountain streams bear the names of saints—Saint Anthony or Saint Bernard's Stream in Maurienne, Saint Marguerite's Stream in Tarentaise—because the "athletes of Christ," as saints were called in the Middle Ages, neutralize the water spirits or limit their power.

Not so long ago, our elders could still tell ethnologists the names of the local spirits, and Charles Joisten gathered an impressive collection of them in the Alps during the 1960s. But now this memory is fading away rapidly as well-being and prosperity no longer depend upon the spirits, but instead upon economic factors. People know where rain and hail comes from, what diseases decimate livestock, and what causes floods. The world has been explored and explained, and stripped of its poetry—alas! People no longer gain control of their property through intimidating rites; they purchase it in the presence of a notary. People no longer go to the fairy fountain; they turn on a faucet. Fortunately, the spirits survive and they emerge from the shadows every time a writer goes back to our roots and does not hesitate to draw inspiration from local beliefs or books from the past. These writers perform a good deed by passing on to us and our children the memory of a bygone world in which spirits were inseparable from humans.

In rediscovering land spirits, we cannot help but notice their modernity. They guided our ancestors to respect their environment and to be careful because they knew they were not alone and had accounts to pay to those who were called—and are still called, here and there—the Invisible Folk and the Underground Folk. Several decades ago, we saw in Iceland that the populace refused to allow a hydroelectrical center to be installed because it was thought it would offend the spirit of the waterfall. Has the disappearance of land spirits not caused catastrophes and given free rein to modern man's presumptuousness? It clearly seems that these spirits formed part of life's regulatory elements and whatever they prove to be, they left us one essential law: mankind should live in harmony with the surrounding nature and treat it as a living being. In order to prosper, then, we must continue to honor the genii loci.

Notes

CHAPTER ONE. UNUSUAL MANIFESTATIONS

1. Giraldus Cambrensis, *Topographia Hibernica,* II, 14.
2. Giraldus Cambrensis, *Itinerarium Cambriae,* II, 7.
3. Nennius, *Historia Brittonum.*
4. Porsia, ed. and trans. *Liber Monstrorum,* I, 34.
5. Cf. Gervase of Tilbury, *Otia Imperialia.*
6. Cited by Walter, *La mémoire du temps,* 494.
7. Cf. Gervase of Tilbury, *Otia Imperialia.*
8. Cf. Maillefer, "Guta saga: Histoire des Gotlandais."
9. Cf. Grimm, *Deutsche Rechtsalterthümer,* 800.
10. Cf. Sébillot, *Le Folklore de France.*
11. Cf. Abry and Abry, "Des Parques aux Fées et autres êtres sauvages."
12. Cf. Dömötör, *Volksglaube und Aberglaube der Ungarn.*
13. Cf. Karlinger and Turczynski, *Rumänische Sagen und Sagen aus Rumänien.*

CHAPTER TWO.
THE FIRST INHABITANTS OF THE EARTH

1. Lecouteux, *Les Monstres dans la littérature allemande de Moyen Age (1150– 1350),* vol. II, 32ff.
2. Map, *De nugis curialium,* I, 1; Ibrahim ben Wasif Shah, *L'Abrégé des merveilles.*

3. On this entire development, see Lecouteux, *Les Monstres,* vol. I, 25ff; and Bresc, "Le Temps des Géants."

4. Cf. Dubost, *Aspects fantastiques de la littérature narrative médiévale (XIIe–XIIIe siècles),* 355ff.

5. Cf. Walter, *La mémoire du temps,* 553; Brereton, ed., *Des Grantz Geanz.*

6. Published in facsimile by J. Heinzle, Göppingen, 1981.

7. Saxo Grammaticus, *The History of the Danes, Books I–IX,* 9 (trans. Fisher).

8. Warnerius of Basel, *Synodicus,* 319–30.

9. Cf. Guyonvarc'h, ed., *Textes mythologiques irlandais I,* vol. II, 1–17.

10. Cf. D'Arbois de Jubainville, *Le Cycle mythologique irlandais et la mythologie celtique,* vol. II, 7; Guyonvarc'h, "La Maladie de Cuchúlainn et l'unique Jalousie d'Emer," 285–306 (see bibliography under *Serglige Con Culainn*).

11. Cf. Giraldus Cambrensis, *Itinerarium Cambriae* I, 8, translation and commentary; Lecouteux and Marcq, *Les esprits et les morts (Essais 13),* 67–71.

12. Cf. Ansbacher, *Die Abschnitte über die Geister und wunderbaren Geschöpfe aus Qazwînî Kosmographie,* 7–28 (partial translation).

13. Cf. D'Arbois de Jubainville, *Le Cycle,* vol. II, 92ff.

CHAPTER THREE. DEMONS AND FALLEN ANGELS

1. For more on this point, see Meeks, *Génies, Anges, Démons.*

2. Meeks, *Génies, Anges, Démons.*

3. Cf. the fine overview by Dando, "The Neutral Angels."

4. Augustine, *City of God,* VII, 33.

5. Martianus Cappella, *De nuptiis Philologiae et Mercurii,* II, 34.

6. Martin de Braga, *De correctione rusticorum,* 7.

7. Quoted in Walter, *La mémoire du temps,* 494.

8. Cf. Lecouteux, "L'arrière-plan des sites aventureux dans le roman médiéval."

9. Giraldus Cambrensis, *Itinerarium Cambriae* I, 12; cf. Lecouteux and Marcq, *Les esprits et les morts,* 45ff.

10. Cf. Lecouteux, "Zwerge und Verwandte," 369.

CHAPTER FOUR. CULT REMNANTS

1. The texts cited in this area of study and their references can be found in Harmening, *Superstitio,* and Boudriot, *Die altgermanische Religion in der*

amtlichen Literatur des Abendlandes vom 5. bis zum 11. Jahrhundert.

2. Caesarius of Arles, *Sermons au Peuple;* Cf. Sermons 1, 12; 13, 5; 14, 4; 54, 5–6.

3. Pirminius, *Dicta Abbatis Pirminii, de singulis libris canonicis scarapsus,* chap. 22.

4. Walter, *La mémoire du temps,* 285.

5. Cf. Clemen, ed., *Fontes historiae religionis Germanicae.*

6. Adam of Bremen, *Gesta ecclesiae Hammaburgensis pontificum,* bk. IV, 26, schol. 138 (134) (trans. Tschan).

7. *De Gloria Confessorum* II, 6 (trans.: Raymond Van Dam); cited by Walter, *Canicule,* 132.

8. *Landnámabók;* Boyer, *Le Livre de la colonisation de l'Islande* (French translation of the most important passages).

9. *Óláfs saga hins Helga,* chap. 15. Cf. Heinrichs, et al., ed. and trans., *Óláfs saga hins Helga: Die "Legendarische Saga" über Olaf den Heiligen.*

10. Tacitus, *Germania,* chap. IX and VII (trans. Rives).

11. Lucan, *Pharsalia,* bk III, 399–413 (trans. Duff).

12. Adam of Bremen, *History of the Archbishops of Hamburg-Bremen,* I, vii; IV, xviii (trans. Tschan).

13. Alcuin in *Vita Sancti Willibrordi,* chap. 10 (trans. Talbot).

14. Cf. Guyonvarc'h and Le Roux, *Les Druides,* 228ff.

15. Cf. Fraikin, "L'Arbre des Fées, le Bois Chenu et la Prophétie de Merlin," 37–46.

CHAPTER FIVE. THE LOCAL LAND SPIRITS

1. Trans. in Jóhannesson, *Íslendinga Saga,* 94. Cf. *Landnámabók,* H 268.

2. *Egil's Saga,* chap. 57 (trans. Pálsson and Edwards).

3. Sturluson, *Heimskringla: The Saga of Óláf Tryggvason,* chap. 33 (trans. Hollander).

4. Vigfússon, *Flateyjarbók,* 1, 420ff.

5. Saxo Grammaticus, *Gesta Danorum,* 286–87.

CHAPTER SIX. THE UNDERSIDE OF IDOLATRY

1. Cf. D'Arbois de Jubainville, *Le Cycle mythologique,* vol. II, 107ff.

2. The inscriptions here are cited by volume and reference number in the *Corpus Inscriptionum Latinorum* (= CIL).

3. Gutenbrunner, *Die germanischen Götternamen der antiken Inschriften.*

4. Cf. Lecouteux and Marcq, *Les esprits et les morts,* 15.

5. Pliny, *Natural History,* XII, 2 (trans. Rackham; punctuation modified).

6. Tacitus, *Germania,* chap. IX (trans. Rives).

7. Ronsard, *Songs & Sonnets of Pierre de Ronsard,* 97.

8. Bede, *Historia ecclesiastica* II, 13. Text in Clemen, *Fontes historiae religionis Germanicae,* 41.

9. Pertz, *Monumenta Germaniae Historica,* SS VII, 5–31.

10. Cf. Knappert, "La Vie de Saint Gall et le paganisme germanique."

11. Knappert, "La Vie de Saint Gall," 276.

12. Cf. Reichert, *Lexikon der altgermanischen Namen* I, 545b (under *Quadriburgi*).

13. CIL 13, 8841.

CHAPTER EIGHT.
SILVANUS AND COMPANY

1. Cf. Pinon, "D'un Dieu gaulois à un Malmédien," esp. 269ff (with a rich bibliography).

2. Lavedan, *Dictionnaire illustré de la mythologie et des antiquités grecques et romaines,* under "Sylvanus."

3. Cf. Walter, *Christian Mythology,* 52–60.

4. Burchard, *Corrector,* 103; cf. Boudriot, *Die altgermanische Religion,* 51.

5. Gervase of Tilbury, *Otia Imperialia,* III, 86.

6. Cf. Lecouteux, "Les Fées au Moyen Age: quelques remarques."

CHAPTER NINE.
THE METAMORPHOSES OF SPIRITS

1. Cf. Lecouteux, *Les Nains et les Elfes au Moyen Age.*

2. Cf. Lecouteux, *Dictionnaire de mythologie germanique,* under "Dises."

3. Both of these texts are cited by Boyer in *Le Monde du Double,* 100, 118.

4. Thórðarson, *Landnámabók, Sturlubók,* 329.

5. Sturluson, *Heimskringla,* chap. 10 (trans. Hollander).

6. Sigal, *L'homme et le miracle dans la France médiévale (XIe–XIIe siècle),* 61.

7. Harmening, "Fränkische Mirakelbücher," 105–6.

8. Sigal, *L'Homme et le miracle*, 62.

9. Ibid., 167–68.

10. Ibid., 169–70.

11. Cf. D'Arbois de Jubainville, *Cours de Littérature celtique*, vol. IV, 214, Triad nr. 14; Loth, *Les Mabinogion*, 91–95 (Story of Branwen, the daughter of Llyr).

12. Feilberg, "Der Kobold in nordischer Überlieferung," 276–77.

13. Lecouteux, "Der Mensch und der Raum am Beispiel der altnordischen Literatur"; "Vom Schrat zum Schrättel: Dämonisierungs-, Mythologisierungs- und Euphemisierungsprozeß einer volkstümlichen Vorstellung."

14. Cf. Boyer, *Sagas islandaises*, 767–960, chapters 32–35.

15. Hermann, *Erläuterungen zu den ersten neun Büchern der Dänischen Geschichte des Saxo Grammaticus*, II: *Kommentar*, 216.

16. Labba, *Anta: les mémoires d'un Lapon*, 470, 476, and 488.

17. Liebrecht, *Zur Volkskunde*, 313.

18. Cf. Bachtold-Stäubli, *Handwörterbuch des deutschen Aberglaubens*, vol. VIII, col. 1465. The full Latin passage reads: *Loca haec vulgus adhuc, unsteten sive loca incerta vocat, de quibus nempe nascitur, ubi sint. Cum enim aliquis huc illucque ambulat et eum vel morbus subito invadit, vel ei membrum aliquod corpori dolet, rationis ignari dicunt, er seye über eine unstete gegangen, sive calcasse eum locum, ubi sit, nesciatur; et quia is sanctis sit, genius loci illum punisse somniatur, tamquam violatorem et contemptatorem sui.*

CHAPTER TEN.
A PROVISIONAL ASSESSMENT

1. Ibn Battûta, *Voyages*, vol. II, 228.

2. Polo, *Description of the World*, vol. I, 140.

CHAPTER ELEVEN.
ENCOUNTERING THE SPIRITS OF THE LOCAL LAND

1. Pertz, *Monumenta Germaniae Historica*, SS VI, 310.

2. Gregory of Tours, *Vita Patrum*, I, 1. Text edition found in *Pertz, Monumenta Germaniae Historica*, SS rer. Merov. 1, 2, 663ff.

3. Martine, *Vie des Pères du Jura*, I, 17.

4. Cf. Sergent, "Traditions scandinaves en Labourd," 6.

5. Le Goff, *Pour un autre Moyen Âge,* 236–79.

6. Delavigne, "Zone inondable: Saints, Géants et Dragons au Nord-Est d'Angers (Maine-et-Loire)," 47–70.

7. Dumont, *La Tarasque: Essai de description d'un fait local d'un point de vue ethnographique.*

8. Peigné-Delacourt, *Les miracles de Saint Éloi,* 110.

9. Cf. Freymond, *Artus' Kampf mit dem Katzenungetüm,* 441ff.

10. Cf. D'Arbois de Jubainville, *Cours de Littérature celtique,* vol. IV, 249.

11. Text in Clemen, *Fontes historiae,* 69.

12. Walter, *La mémoire du temps,* 552.

13. Text in Clemen, *Fontes historiae,* 73.

CHAPTER TWELVE.
TAKING POSSESSION OF A PIECE OF LAND

1. Cited by Faral, *La Légende arthurienne,* vol. I, 241ff.

2. Gelis, "La Sainte de Viserny," 11–15.

3. Cf., for example, Fromage, "Les Aspects celtiques du personnage de saint Denys," 15–27.

4. Cf. Sigal, *L'homme et le miracle,* 61ff.

5. Guériff, "Guérande et le culte de saint Michel," 7.

6. Giraldus Cambrensis, *Topographia Hibernica,* II, 28.

7. Jacobus de Voragine, *Legenda Aurea,* "De Sancto Michaele Archangelo." For the Latin edition, see bibliography under Iacopo da Varazze.

8. Walter, *Christian Mythology,* 162–63.

9. Cf. Barre, "Notre-Dame-de-Bon-Encontre, près d'Agen."

10. Thórðarson, *Landnámabók, Sturlubók,* 29.

11. *Laxdæla Saga,* chap. 17.

12. These have been meticulously studied in Strömbäck, "Att helga land."

13. Thórðarson, *Landnámabók, Sturlubók,* 184.

14. Grimm, *Deutsche Rechtsalterthümer,* 545.

15. Maillefer, "Guta saga," 132.

16. Grimm, *Deutsche Rechtsalterthümer,* 55ff.

17. Ibid., 57.

18. Cf. Boyer, *Le Livre de la colonisation,* 118–21.

CHAPTER THIRTEEN.
CIRCUMAMBULATION: APPROPRIATION, EXPROPRIATION, AND PROTECTION RITES

1. Eliade, *Cosmos and History: Myth of the Eternal Return,* 15–16.
2. Delpech, "Rite, légende, mythe et société: fondations et fondateurs dans la tradition folklorique de la peninsule ibérique," 27ff.
3. Dumézil, *Rituels indo-européens à Rome,* 27ff.
4. Eliade, *Cosmos and History,* 16.
5. Jónsson, ed., *Edda Snorra Sturlusonar.*
6. Cf. Sturluson, *Heimskringla, Ynglingasaga,* chap. 5 (trans. Hollander).
7. Le Duc, ed., *Vie de Saint-Malo, évêque d'Alet,* chap. 34.
8. Vries, *Altgermanische Religionsgeshichte,* vol. I, 386.
9. Jacobus de Voragine, *Legenda Aurea,* "De Litaniis." For the Latin edition, see bibliography under Iacopo da Varazze.
10. Cf. Scott, *Histoire de la démonologie et de la sorcellerie,* 252.
11. Nordal and Jónsson, *Borgfirðinga Sögur,* chap. 9.
12. Sturluson, *Heimskringla,* chap. 203 (trans. Hollander). My emphasis.
13. Cf. Laurent's excellent study, "Le Juste Milieu. Réflexion sur un ritual de circumambulation millénaire: La Troménie de Locronan," esp. 279ff.
14. Dumézil, *Rituels indo-européens à Rome,* 28ff.
15. Cf. Scheid and Svenbro, "Byrsa, la ruse d'Elissa et la foundation de Carthage."
16. The English here is based on the translation by Michèle Perret of D'Arras, *Le roman de Mélusine ou L'histoire des Lusignan.*
17. Coudrette, *Le Roman de Mélusine ou Histoire de Lusignan,* verse 897ff. I am also using the Middle High German *Melusine* by Thüring von Ringoltingen.
18. Eliade, *Cosmos and History,* 9–10.

CHAPTER FOURTEEN.
BOUNDARIES AND THEIR MARKERS

1. For the full development of this, cf. Grimm, *Deutsche Rechtsalterthümer,* II, 71–77.
2. Cf. Greimas, *Of Gods and Men: Studies in Lithuanian Mythology,* 39, and cf. also 30–31.
3. For the original text, see Ewert, ed., *Gui de Warewic.*

CHAPTER FIFTEEN.
THE ENCLOSED SPACE IS SACRED

1. Pertz in *Monumenta Germaniae Historica,* SS V, 812, 816.
2. Cf. Maillefer, "Guta saga," 134.
3. Sturluson, *Heimskringla,* chap. 133 (trans. Hollander).
4. Rives translation.

CHAPTER SIXTEEN.
THE CONTRACT WITH THE SPIRITS

1. Cf. Bächtold-Stäubli, *Handwörterbuch des deutschen Aberglaubens,* vol. X, under "Bauopfer"; and Klausemann, *Das Bauopfer.*
2. Faral, *La Légende arthurienne,* vol. III.
3. Guest, trans., *The Mabinogion,* 92–93.
4. Cf., for example, Vadé, "Le Système des Mediolanum en Gaule"; Guyonvarc'h and Le Roux, *Les Druides,* 217ff.
5. Cf. the magisterial study by Taloş, *Meşterud Manole: Contributie la studiul unei teme de folclor european.* I would like to thank Ion Taloş for sending me his fine book.
6. Cf. Liungman, "Das Rå und der Herr der Tiere."
7. Sébillot, *Le Folklore de France,* vol. IV, 89ff.
8. Cf. Liebrecht, *Zur Volkskunde,* 258.
9. Cf. Pradel, "Der Schatten im Volksglauben"; Negelein, "Bild, Spiegel und Schatten im Volksglauben."
10. *Kristni Saga,* chap. 2 (trans. Grønlie).
11. Cf. *Þáttr Þorvalds ens Víðförla* in Jónsson, ed., *Islendingasögur* VII, 437–63.
12. These and many other accounts can be found in Feilberg, "Der Kobold in nordischer Überlieferung."
13. Cf. Liungman, "Das Rå und der Herr der Tiere."
14. Cf. Jouet, *Religion et Mythologie des Baltes: Une tradition indo-européene.*
15. Cf. Feilberg, "Der Kobold in nordischer Überlieferung."

CHAPTER SEVENTEEN.
THE CIRCULAR AND THE RECTAGULAR:
A HYPOTHESIS

1. Dumézil, *Rituels indo-européens à Rome*. This book provides some useful bibliographical references.
2. Marquardt, *Le culte chez les Romains,* 187–88.
3. Dumézil, *Rituels indo-européens à Rome,* 33.
4. Cf. Ovid, *Fasti,* bk. VI, 266–82.
5. Vernant, *Mythe et Pensée chex les Grecs,* 149.
6. Cf. Vries, *Altgermanische Religionsgeshichte,* vol. I, 277ff.
7. Cf. Thümmel's important study, "Der germanische Tempel," with plan diagrams.

CHAPTER EIGHTEEN.
THE CONQUEST OF THE SPACE

1. Vries, *Altgermanische Religionsgeshichte,* vol. II, index of theophoric names.
2. More ample references can be found in Lecouteux, "Der Mensch und der Raum am Beispiel der altnordischen Literatur."

CHAPTER NINETEEN.
WATERS, SPRINGS, AND FOUNTAINS

1. Cf. Lecouteux, "L'arrière-plan mythique des sites aventureux dans le roman médiéval."
2. Cf. Thompson, *The Elucidation,* 29ff.
3. Cited by Gallais, *La Fée à l'arbre et à la fontaine,* 28.
4. Cited by Walter, *Canicule,* 78.
5. See Gallais, *La Fée à l'arbre.*
6. Cf. Lecouteux, *Mélusine et le Chevalier au cygne.*
7. Harf-Lancner, "Une Mélusine galloise: La Dame du lac de Brecknock."
8. Walter, *Canicule,* 121.
9. Ibid., 123–24.
10. Ibid., 137–38.
11. Micha, *Lancelot,* 76, 1ff.

12. Roussineau, *Perceforest,* IV, 40.

13. Aymon de Varennes, *Florimont.*

14. Cf. Gallais, *La Fée à l'arbre,* 316.

15. Breuer, *Cristal et Clarie.*

16. Cf. Lecouteux, *Les Nains et les Elfes au Moyen Age.*

17. Brunel, ed., *Jaufré: Roman arthurien du XIIIe siècle en vers provençaux,* verse 8327ff.

18. Cf. Gallais, *La Fée à l'arbre,* 274.

19. Ibid., 259–60.

CHAPTER TWENTY. THE FOREST

1. Sommer, *The Vulgate Version of the Arthurian Romances,* vol. II.

2. Ibid.

3. Micha, *Étude sur le "Merlin" de Robert de Boron,* 149.

4. Faral, *La Légende arthurienne,* vol. II, 45. The text, taken from the *Vie des Pères* (mid-thirteenth century) was edited by Méon in *Nouveau recueil de fabliaux et contes inédits des poètes français des XIIe, XIIIe, XIVe et XVe siècles,* vol. II, 236–55.

5. Original text and French translation in Ruelle, ed., *Huon de Bordeaux.*

6. Cf. Lecouteux, *Les Nains et les Elfes au Moyen Age.*

CHAPTER TWENTY-ONE. THE MOUNTAIN AND ITS SPIRITS

1. Cf. Lecouteux, "Aspects mythiques de la montagne au Moyen Age."

2. *Ratio de cathecizandis rudibus* (see bibliography for full edition); cited by Harmening, *Superstitio,* 247.

3. Gervase of Tilbury, *Otia Imperialia,* III, 43 and 58.

4. Cf., for example, Marliave, *Petit dictionnaire de mythologies basque et pyrénéenne.*

5. Cf. Dubost, *Aspects fantastiques,* 459–62.

6. Ibid., 462.

7. Subrenat, ed., *Le Roman d'Auberon.*

8. Brandin, ed., *La Chanson d'Aspremont.*

9. Couraye du Parc, ed., *La Mort Aymeri de Narbonne.*

10. Martin, ed., *Fergus: Roman von Guillaume le Clerc.*

11. Dubost, *Aspects fantastiques,* 473.

12. Guest, trans., *The Mabinogion,* 201.

13. Cf. the chapters devoted to saints, dragons, and dwarves in Lecouteux, *Les Monstres dans la littérature allemande du Moyen Âge (1150–1350).*

CHAPTER TWENTY-TWO.
THE PROBLEM OF *PARÉDRIE*

1. Dontenville, *Histoire et Géographie mythiques de la France,* 126ff; Dubost, *Aspects fantastiques,* 481–86.

2. Cf. Lecouteux, *La Légende de Siegfried.*

3. Greimas, *Of Gods and Men,* 95.

CHAPTER TWENTY-THREE.
A COMPOSITE SITE:
THE DWELLING OF GRENDEL AND HIS MOTHER

1. For this text I have consulted the diplomatic edition of *Beowulf,* with French translation and commentary by André Crépin.

2. The translation of this section, slightly augmented, is from Lehmann, trans., *Beowulf.*

3. Lehmann, trans., *Beowulf.*

4. Cf. Lecouteux, *The Return of the Dead.*

5. Konrad von Stoffeln, *Gauriel von Muntabel,* ed. Khull.

CHAPTER TWENTY-FOUR. THE MOOR

1. Brandin, ed., *Fouke Fitz Warin.* The sections given here appear on pp. 3–7.

CHAPTER TWENTY-FIVE.
THE HYBRIDIZATION OF MYTHS

1. Wirnt von Grafenberg, *Wigalois, der Ritter mit dem Rade,* ed. Kapteyn.

Bibliography

Abry, Christian, and Dominique Abry. "Des Parques aux Fées et autres êtres sauvages: 'Naroues' (XVIe s.), 'Naroves' (XIXe s.), and 'Naroua' (XXe s.) savoyardes." *Le Monde alpin et rhodanien* 1–4 (1982): 247–80.

Adam of Bremen. *Gesta ecclesiae Hammaburgensis pontificum* IV. Edited by B. Schmeidler. Hannover: Hahn, 1917.

———. *History of the Archbishops of Hamburg-Bremen.* Translated by Francis J. Tschan. New York: Columbia University Press, 1959.

Ansbacher, Jonas. *Die Abschnitte über die Geister und wunderbaren Geschöpfe aus Qazwînî's Kosmographie.* Dissertation. Friedrich-Alexanders-Universität, Erlangen, 1905.

Aymon de Varennes. *Florimont.* Edited by Alfons Hilka. Göttingen: Gesellschaft für romanische Literatur, 1933.

Augustine. *City of God.* Translated by Marcus Dods. In *Nicene and Post-Nicene Fathers,* First Series, vol. 2. Edited by Philip Schaff. Buffalo, N.Y.: Christian Literature Publishing Co., 1887.

Bachtold-Stäubli, Hans. *Handwörterbuch des deutschen Aberglaubens.* 10 vols. Berlin and New York: De Gruyter, 1987.

Barre, André. "Notre-Dame-de-Bon-Encontre, près d'Agen." *Mythologie française* 142 (1987): 19–24.

Battûta, Ibn. *Voyages.* Translated by C. Defremery and B. R. Sanguinetti. 3 vols. Paris: Maspero, 1982.

Bede. *Historia ecclesiastica.* In *Fontes historiae religionis Germanicae.* Edited by Carolus Clemen. Berlin: De Gruyter, 1928.

Benediktsson, Jakob, ed. *Íslendingabók—Landnámabók*. Íslenzk Fornrit I. Reykjavik: Hið íslenzka fornritafélag, 1968.

Beowulf. Diplomatic edition, translated with commentary by André Crépin. 2 vols. Göppingen: Kümmerle, 1991.

Boudriot, Wilhelm. *Die altgermanische Religion in der amtlichen Literatur des Abendlandes vom 5. bis zum 11. Jahrhundert*. Bonn: Röhrscheid, 1928.

Boyer, Régis. *Le Livre de la colonisation de l'Islande*. Paris: De Gruyter, 1973.

———. *Le Monde du Double. La magie chez les anciens Scandinaves*. Paris: Berg, 1986.

———. *Sagas islandaises*. Paris: Gallimard, 1987.

Brandin, Louis, ed. *Folke Fitz Warin*. Paris: Champion, 1930.

———, ed. *La Chanson d'Aspremont*. 2 vols. Paris: Champion, 1923–1924.

Brereton, Georgine E., ed. *Des Grantz Geanz*. Oxford: Oxford University Press, 1937.

Bresc, Henri. "Le Temps des Géants." In *Temps, mémoire, tradition au Moyen Age: actes du XIIIe congrès de la Société des historiens médiévistes de l'enseignement supérieur public, Aix-en-Provence, 4–5 juin 1982*. Aix-en-Provence: Université de Provence, 1983, 245–65.

Breuer, Hermann, ed. *Cristal und Clarie*. Dresden: Gesellschaft für romanische Literatur, 1915.

Brunel, Clovis, ed. *Jaufré: Roman arthurien du XIIIe siècle en vers provençaux*. 2 vols. Paris: Société des anciens textes français, 1943.

Burchard of Worms. *Corrector*. In *Decretum*. N.p. ca. 1008–1012.

Caesarius of Arles. *Sermons au Peuple*. Edited and translated by Marie-José Delage, 2 vols. Paris: Cerf, 1971–1978.

Chrétien de Troyes. *Le Roman de Perceval ou Le Conte du Graal. Edition critique d'après tous les manuscrits*. Edited by Keith Busby. Berlin: De Gruyter, 1993.

Clemen, Carolus, ed. *Fontes historiae religionis Germanicae*. Berlin: De Gruyter, 1928.

Corpus Inscriptionum Latinarum. Berlin-Brandenburg Academy of Sciences and Humanities, 1853–present.

Coudrette. *Le Roman de Mélusine ou Histoire de Lusignan*. Edited by Eleanor Roach. Paris: Klincksieck, 1982.

Couraye du Parc, Joseph, ed. *La Mort Aymeri de Narbonne*. Paris: Didot, 1884.

Dando, Marcel. "The Neutral Angels." *Archiv für das Studium der neueren Sprachen und Literaturen* 217 (1980): 259–76.

D'Arbois de Jubainville, Marie-Henri. *Cours de Littérature celtique,* vol. IV. Paris: Thorin, 1889.

———. *Le Cycle mythologique irlandais et la mythologie celtique,* vol. II. Paris: Thorin, 1884.

D'Arras, Jean. *Le roman de Mélusine ou L'histoire des Lusignan.* Translated by Michèle Perret. Paris: Stock, 1979.

Delavigne, Raymond. "Zone inondable: Saints, Géants et Dragons au Nord-Est d'Angers (Maine-et-Loire)." *Mythologie française* 117 (1980): 47–70.

Delpech, François. "Rite, légende, mythe et société: fondations et fondateurs dans la tradition folklorique de la péninsule ibérique." *Medieval Folklore* 1 (1991): 10–56.

Dömötör, Tekla. *Volksglaube und Aberglaube der Ungarn.* Budapest: Kiadó, 1982.

Dontenville, Henri. *Histoire et Géographie mythiques de la France.* Paris: Maisonneuve and La Rose, 1973.

Dubost, Francis. *Aspects fantastiques de la littérature narrative médiévale (XIIe–XIIIe siècles): L'autre, l'ailleurs, l'autrefois.* 2 vols. Paris: Champion, 1991.

Dumézil, Georges, *Rituels indo-européens à Rome.* Paris: Klincksieck, 1954.

Dumont, Louis. *La Tarasque: Essai de description d'un fait local d'un point de vue ethnographique.* Paris: Gallimard, 1951.

Egil's Saga. Translated by Hermann Pálsson and Paul Edwards. London: Penguin, 1976.

Eliade, Mircea. *Cosmos and History: Myth of the Eternal Return.* Translated by Willard R. Trask. New York: Harper & Brothers, 1959.

Ewert, Alfred, ed. *Gui de Warewic.* 2 vols. Paris: Champion, 1933.

Faral, Edmond. *La Légende arthurienne.* Paris: Champion, 1929.

Feilberg, H. F. "Der Kobold in nordischer Überlieferung." *Zeitschrift des Vereins für Volkskunde* 8 (1898): 1–20, 130–46, 264–77.

Fraikin, Jean. "L'Arbre des Fées, le Bois Chenu et la Prophétie de Merlin." *Mythologie française* 147–49 (1987): 37–46.

Franco, Isabelle. *Rites et Croyances d'éternité.* Paris: Pygmalion, 1993.

Freymond, Émile. *Artus' Kampf mit dem Katzenungetüm: Eine Episode der Vulgata des Livre d'Artus, die Sage und ihre Lokaliserung in Savoyen.* Halle: Niemeyer, 1899.

Fromage, Henri. "Les Aspects celtiques du personnage de saint Denis." *Mythologie française* 144 (1987): 15–27.

Gallais, Pierre. *La Fée à l'arbre et à la fontaine: un archétype du conte merveilleux et du récit courtois.* Amsterdam and Atlanta: Rodopi, 1992.

Gelis, Jacques. "La Sainte de Viserny. Le Culte de sainte Christine et la Mythologie sacrée de Viserny (Côte-d'Or)." *Mythologie française* 147–49 (1987): 11–15.

Gervase of Tilbury. *Otia Imperialia: Recreation for an Emperor.* Edited and translated by S. E. Banks and J. W. Binns. Oxford: Oxford University Press, 2002. French edition: *Le Livre des merveilles.* Translated by Annie Duchesne. Paris: Les Belles Lettres, 1992.

Giraldus Cambrensis [Gerald of Wales]. *Itinerarium Cambriae.* Edited by James F. Dimock. London: Longman, Green, Reader, and Dyer, 1868.

———. *Topographia Hibernica et Expugnatio Hibernica.* Edited by James F. Dimock. London: Longmans, Green, Reader and Dyer, 1867.

Grafenberg, Wirnt von. *Wigalois, der Ritter mit dem Rade.* Edited by J. M. N. Kapteyn. Bonn: Klopp, 1926. French translation by Claude Lecouteux and Véronique Lévy. *Wigalois, le chevalier à la Roue.* Grenoble: ELLUG, 2001.

Gregory of Tours. *Glory of the Confessors.* Translated by Raymond Van Dam. Liverpool: Liverpool University Press, 1988.

Greimas, Algirdas J. *Of Gods and Men: Studies in Lithuanian Mythology.* Translated by Milda Newman. Bloomington and Indiana: Indiana University Press, 1992.

Grimm, Jacob. *Deutsche Rechtsalterthümer.* 2nd ed. Göttingen: Dieterich, 1854.

Guériff, Fernand. "Guérande et le culte de saint Michel." *Mythologie française* 160 (1991): 5–11.

Guest, Lady Charlotte, trans. *The Mabinogion.* London: Dent, 1910.

Guillaume le Clerc. *Fergus.* Edited by E. Martin. Halle: Waisenhaus, 1872.

Gutenbrunner, Siegfried. *Die germanischen Götternamen der antiken Inschriften.* Halle: Niemeyer, 1936.

Guyonvarc'h, Christian, ed. *Textes mythologiques irlandais I.* Rennes: Ogam, 1980.

Guyonvarc'h, Christian J., and Françoise Le Roux. *Les Druides.* Rennes: Editions Ouest, 1986.

Harf-Lancner, Laurence. "Une Melusine galloise: La Dame du lac de Brecknock." In *Mélanges Jeanne Lods.* Paris: Presses de l'ENSJF, 1978, 323–38.

Harmening, Dieter. "Frankische Mirakelbücher: Quellen und Untersuchungen zur historischen Volkskunde und Geschichte der Volksfrömmigkeit." *Würzburger Diözesangeshichtsblätter* 28 (1966): 25–240.

———. *Superstitio*. Berlin: Schmidt, 1979.

Heinrichs, Anne, et al, ed. and trans. *Óláfs saga hins Helga: Die "Legendarische Saga" über Olaf den Heiligen (Hs. Delagard. saml. nr. 8 II)*. Heidelberg: Winter, 1982.

Heldenbuch. Facsimile of the oldest printed edition, edited by Joachim Heinzle. Göppingen: Kummerle, 1981.

Hermann, Paul. *Erläuterungen zu den ersten neun Büchern der Dänischen Geschichte des Saxo Grammaticus,* vol. II: *Kommentar.* Leipzig: Engelmann, 1922.

Homilia de sacrilegiis. In *Eine Augustin fälschlich beigelegte Homilia de sacrilegiis*. Edited by C. P. Caspari. Christiania [Oslo]: Dybwad/Brügger, 1886.

Ibrahim ben Wasif Shah. *L'Abrégé des merveilles*. Translated by Baron Carra de Vaux. Paris: Klincksieck, 1898. Reprint Paris: Sindbad, 1984.

Iacopo da Varazze [Jacobus de Voragine]. *Legenda Aurea*. Edited by Giovanni Paolo Maggioni. 2nd ed. 2 vols. Florence: SISMEL/Edizioni del Galluzzo, 1998.

Jóhannesson, Jón. *Íslendinga Saga: A History of the Old Icelandic Commonwealth*. Translated by Haraldur Bessason. Winnipeg: University of Manitoba Press, 1974.

Jónsson, Finnur, ed. *Edda Snorra Sturlusonar*. Copenhagen: Gyldendal, 1931.

Jónsson, Guðni, ed. *Kristni saga*. In *Íslendinga sögur I: Landssaga og Landnám*. Reykjavik: Íslendíngasagnaútgáfan, 1954.

———, ed. *Þáttr Þorvalds ens Víðförla*. In *Íslendingasögur VII*. Reykjavik: Íslendíngasagnaútgáfan, 1946.

Jouet, Philippe. *Religion et Mythologie des Baltes: Une tradition indo-européene*. Paris and Milan: Archè, 1989.

Karlinger Felix, and Turczynski, E. *Rumänische Sagen und Sagen aus Rumänien*. Berlin: Schmidt, 1982.

Klausemann, Kurt. *Das Bauopfer: Eine ethnographisch-prähistorisch-linguistische Studie*. Graz and Hamburg: self-published, 1919.

Knappert, Laurentius. "La Vie de Saint Gall et le paganisme germanique." *Revue de l'Histoire des Religions* 29 (1884): 259–95.

Konrad von Stoffeln. *Gauriel von Muntabel: eine höfische Erzählung aus dem 13. Jahrhundert*. Edited by Ferdinand Khull. Graz: Leuschner und Lubensky 1885.

Kristni saga. In *Íslendingabók—Kristni Saga: The Book of the Icelanders—The Story of the Conversion*. Translated by Siân Grønlie. London: Viking Society for Northern Research, 2006.

Labba, Andreas. *Anta: les mémoires d'un Lapon*. Paris: Plon, 1989.

Laurent, Donatien. "Le Juste Milieu. Réflexion sur un rituel de circumambulation millénaire: La Troménie de Locronan." In *Tradition et Histoire dans la culture populaire: Rencontres autour de l'œuvre de Jean-Michel Guilcher, Grenoble, Musée dauphinois, 20–21 janvier 1989*. Grenoble: Centre Alpin et Rhodanien d'Ethnologie, 1990, 25–92.

Lavedan, Pierre. *Dictionnaire illustré de la mythologie et des antiquités grecques et romaines*. Paris: Brodard et Taupin, 1932.

Laxdoela saga. Translated by Muriel A. C. Press. Project Gutenberg, ca. 1245.

Lecouteux, Claude. "Aspects mythiques de la montagne au Moyen Age." In *Le Monde alpin et rhodanien 1–4* (1982): 43–54.

———. "Der Mensch und der Raum am Beispiel der altnordischen Literatur." *Euphorion* 85 (1991): 224–34.

———. Aspects de la forêt dans les traditions germaniques. *Mythes, symboles et langues* 2 (Nagoya, 2009) : 7-20.

———. "La terre apprivoisée : quelques réflexions sur l'homme et son milieu," in *Tradition et histoire dans la culture populaire*, pp. 293–97. Grenoble, 1990 (Documents d'Ethnologie régionale 11).

———. *La légende de Siegfried*. Paris: Le Porte-Glaive, 1995.

———. "L'arrière-plan des sites aventureux dans le roman médiéval." *Études germaniques* 41 (1991): 293–304.

———. "Les Fées au Moyen Age: quelques remarques." *Mythologie française* 146 (1987): 26–31.

———. "Les monstres norrois, quelques remarques." In *Deformierte Körper*, t. 2: Die Wahrnehmung und das Andere im Mittelalter, edited by Gabriela Antunes, Björn Reich, and Carmen Stange, 225–40. Göttingen: Universitätsverlag, 2014.

———. *Les Monstres dans la littérature allemande de Moyen Age (1150–1350)*. 3 vols. Göppingen: Kümmerle, 1982.

———. *Les Nains et les Elfes au Moyen Age*. Paris: Imago, 1988.

———. *Mélusine et le Chevalier au cygne*. Paris: Payot, 1982.

———. *Dictionnaire de mythologie germanique*. 3rd ed. Paris: Imago, 2014.

———. *The Return of the Dead*. Rochester, Vt.: Inner Traditions, 2009.

———. "Vom Schrat zum Schrättel: Dämonisierungs-, Mythologisierungs- und Euphemisierungsprozeß einer volkstümlichen Vorstellung." *Euphorion* 79 (1985): 95–108.

———. "Zwerge und Verwandte." *Euphorion* 75 (1981): 366–78.

Lecouteux, Claude, and Philippe Marcq. *Les esprits et les morts.* Paris: Champion, 1990.

Lecouteux, Claude, trans. *La Légende de Siegfried d'après La Chanson Seyfried à la Peau de corne et La Saga de Thidrek de Verone.* Paris: Porte-Glaive, 1994.

Le Duc, Gwenaël, ed. and trans. *Vie de Saint-Malo, évêque d'Alet.* Rennes: Ce.R.A.A., 1979.

Le Goff, Jacques. *Pour un autre Moyen Âge. Temps, travail et culture en Occident: dix-huit essais.* Paris: Gallimard, 1977.

Lehmann, Ruth P., trans. *Beowulf.* Austin: University of Texas Press, 1988.

Liebrecht, Felix. *Zur Volkskunde.* Heilbronn: Henninger, 1879.

Liungman, Waldemar. "Das Rå und der Herr der Tiere." In *The Supernatural Owners of Nature: Nordic Symposium on the Religious Conception of Ruling Spirits (Genii Loci, Genii Speciei) and Allied Concepts,* edited by Åke Hultkrantz, pp. 72–90. Stockholm, Gothenburg, and Uppsala: Almqvist & Wiksell, 1961.

Loth, Joseph. *Les Mabinogion.* Paris: Thorin, 1889.

———. *Les Mabinogion.* 2nd ed. Paris: Les Presses d'Aujourd'hui, 1979.

Lucan. *The Civil War Books I–X (Pharsalia).* Latin text with English translation by J. D. Duff. Cambridge, Mass.: Harvard University Press, 1962.

Maillefer, Jean, trans. "Guta saga: Histoire des Gotlandais. Introduction, traduction, commentaires." *Études germaniques* 40 (1985): 131–40.

Map, Walter. *De nugis curialium.* Edited by M. R. James. Oxford: Oxford University Press, 1914.

Marliave, Olivier de. *Petit dictionnaire de mythologies basque et pyrénéenne.* Paris: Entente, 1993.

Marquardt, Karl Joachim. *Le culte chez les Romains.* Paris: Thorin, 1889.

Martianus Capella. *De nuptiis Philologiae et Mercurii, et de septem artibus liberalibus libri novem.* Edited by Ulrich Friedrich Kopp. Frankfurt am Main: Varrentrap, 1836.

Martin de Braga. *De correctione rusticorum.* Edited by Carl Paul Caspari, Christiania [Oslo]: Malling, 1883.

Martin, Ernst, ed. *Fergus: Roman von Guillaume le Clerc.* Halle: Waisenhaus, 1872.

Martine, François. *Vie des Pères du Jura.* Paris: Cerf, 1968.

Meeks, Dimitri, et al. *Génies, Anges, Démons.* Paris: Éditions du Seuil, 1971.

Méon, Dominique Martin, ed. *Nouveau recueil de fabliaux et contes inédits des poètes français des XIIe, XIIIe, XIVe et XVe siècles,* vol. II. Paris: Chasseriau, 1823.

Micha, Alexandre, ed. *Lancelot.* 9 vols. Paris: Droz, 1978–1983.

———. *Étude sur le "Merlin" de Robert de Boron: roman du XIIIe siècle.* Geneva: Droz, 1980.

Moule, Paul Pelliot, and Louis Hambis. *Le Devisement du monde.* Paris: La Découverte, 1983.

Negelein, Julius von. "Bild, Spiegel und Schatten im Volksglauben." *Archiv für Religionswissenschaft* 5/1 (1902): 1–37.

Nennius. *Historia Brittonum.* In *La Légende arthurienne: études et documents,* vol. 1. Edited by Edmond Faral. Paris: Champion, 1969.

Nordal, Sigurður, et al., eds. *Flateyjarbók.* 4 vols. Akranes: Flateyjarútgáfan, 1944–1945.

Nordal, Sigurður, and Guðni Jónsson, eds. *Borgfirðinga Sögur.* Íslenzk Fornrit III. Reykjavik: Hið íslenzka fornritafélag, 1938.

Ovid. *Ovid's Fasti.* With a translation by Sir James George Frazer. Cambridge, Mass.: Harvard University Press, 1959.

Peigné-Delacourt, Achilles, ed. *Les miracles de Saint Éloi: Poème du XIIIe siècle.* Paris: Aubry, 1859.

Pertz, George Heinrich. *Monumenta Germaniae Historica,* SS VII. Hannover: Hahn, 1829.

Pinon, Roger. "D'un Dieu gaulois à un Malmédien. Etymologie et Sémantique de *dûhon*." *Ollodagos* 3 (1992): 237–306.

Pliny. *Natural History,* vol. XII. Translated by H. Rackham. Cambridge, Mass.: Heinemann and Harvard, 1960.

Polo, Marco. *The Description of the World.* Translated by A. C. Moule and Paul Pelliot. 2 vols. London: Routledge & Sons, 1938.

Porsia, Franco, ed. and trans. *Liber Monstrorum.* Bari: Dedalo, 1976.

Pirminius [Saint Pirmin]. *Dicta Abbatis Pirminii, de singulis libris canonicis scarapsus.* In G. Jecker, "Die Heimat des hl. Pirmin des Apostels der Alamanen." *Beiträge zur Geschichte des alten Mönchtums und des Benediktinerordens* 13 (1927): 34–73.

Pradel, F. "Der Schatten im Volksglauben." *Mitteilungen der schlesischen Gesellschaft für Volkskunde* 12 (1904): 1–36.

Ratio de cathecizandis rudibus. In *Ein karolingischer Missionskatechismus: Ratio de cathecizandis rudibus und die Tauf-Katechesen des Maxentius von Aquileia and eines Anonymus in Kodex Emmeram.* Edited by Joseph Michael Heer. Freiburg: Herder, 1911.

Reichert, Hermann, and Willibald Kraml. *Lexikon der altgermanischen Namen.* 2 vols. Vienna: Österreichische Akademie der Wissenschaften, 1987–1990.

Robert de Boron. *Merlin.* Edited by Alexander Micha. Paris: Champion, 1980.

Ronsard, Pierre de. *To the Woodsman of Gastine.* In *Songs & Sonnets of Pierre de Ronsard Gentleman of Vendomois.* Translated by Curtis Hidden Page. Boston and New York: Houghton Mifflin, 1903.

Roussineau, Gilles, ed. *Perceforest.* 2 vols. Paris: Champion, 1987.

Ruelle, Pierre, ed. *Huon de Bordeax.* Translation by F. Suard. Paris: Flammarion, 1983.

Saxo Grammaticus. *Saxonis Grammatici Gesta Danorum.* Edited by Alfred Holder. Strassburg: Trübner, 1886. English edition: Saxo Grammaticus, *The History of the Danes, Books I–IX.* Edited by Hilda Ellis Davidson and translated by Peter Fisher. Cambridge: Brewer, 1996.

Scheid, John, and Jesper Svenbro. "Byrsa, la ruse d'Elissa et la foundation de Carthage." *Annales E.S.C.* 2 (1985): 328–42.

Sébillot, Paul. *Le Folklore de France.* 4 vols. Paris: Imago, 1968 [1906].

Sergent, Bernard. "Traditions scandinaves en Labourd." *Mythologie française* 163 (1992): 5–9.

Serglige Con Culainn. English translation by Miles Dillon, "The Wasting Sickness of Cú Chulainn." *Scottish Gaelic Studies* 7 (1953): 47–88. French translation by Christian Guyonvarc'h. "La Maladie de Cuchúlainn et l'unique Jalousie d'Emer." *Ogam* 10 (1958): 285–306.

Scott, Walter. *Letters on Demonology and Witchcraft, Addressed to J. G. Lockhart, Esq.* London: Murray, 1930. French edition: *Histoire de la démonologie et de la sorcellerie dédiée à J. G. Lockhart.* Paris: Furne, 1832.

Sigal, Pierre-André. *L'homme et le miracle dans la France médiévale (XIe–XIIe siècle).* Paris: Cerf, 1985.

Sommer, H. Oskar, ed. *Le Livre d'Artus.* In *The Vulgate Version of the Arthurian Romances,* vol. VII. Washington, D.C.: Carnegie Institution of Washington, 1913.

————, ed. *Merlin-Vulgate* in *The Vulgate Version of the Arthurian Romances,* vol. II. Washington D.C.: Carnegie Institution of Washington, 1908.

Strömbäck, Dag. "Att helga land: Studier i Landnáma och det äldste rituella besittningstagandet." In *Festskrift tillägnad Axel Hägerström den 6 september 1928,* pp. 198–220. Uppsala: Almqvist & Wiksell, 1928.

Sturluson, Snorri. *Heimskringla.* Edited by Bjarni Aðalbjarnarson. Íslenzk Fornrit 26 and 28. 2 vols. Reykjavik: Hið íslenzka fornritafélag, 1941–1951.

————. *Heimskringla: The Saga of Oláf Tryggvason.* Translated by Lee M. Hollander. Austin: University of Texas, 1964.

————. *La Saga des Ynglingar.* Translated by Ingeborg Cavalié. Paris: Aubier, 1990.

————. *La Saga d'Oláf Tryggvason.* Translated by Régis Boyer. Paris: Payot, 1992.

Subrenat, Jean, ed. *Le Roman d'Auberon.* Geneva and Paris: Droz/Minard, 1973.

Tacitus. *Germania.* Translated by J. B. Rives. Oxford: Oxford University Press, 1999.

Talbot, C. H., trans. *The Anglo-Saxon Missionaries in Germany: Being the Lives of SS. Willibrord, Boniface, Sturm, Leoba and Lebuin, Together with the Hodeporicon of St. Willibald and a Selection from the Correspondence of St. Boniface.* London: Sheed & Ward, 1954.

Taloş, Ion. *Meşterud Manole: Contributie la studiul unei teme de folclor european.* 2 vols. Bucharest: Minerva, 1973–1997.

Thompson, Albert Wilder. *The Elucidation: A Prologue to the Conte del Graal.* New York: Institute of French Studies, 1931.

Thórðarson, Sturla. *Landnámabók, Sturlubók.* N.p. N.d.

Thümmel, Albert. "Der germanische Tempel." *Beiträge zur Geschichte der deutschen Sprache und Literatur* 35 (1909): 1–123.

Thüring von Ringoltingen. *Melusine.* Edited by Karin Schneider. Berlin: Schmidt, 1958.

Vadé, Yves. "Le Système des Mediolanum en Gaule." *Mythologie française* 163 (1992): 17–30.

Vernant, Jean-Pierre. *Mythe et Pensée chex les Grecs.* Paris: Maspero, 1980.

Vigfússon, Guðbrandur. *Flateyjarbók.* Edited by Carl Rikard. Christiania: P. T. Malling, 1868.

Vries, Jan de. *Altgermanische Religiongeschichte.* 2 vols. Berlin: De Gruyter, 1956.

Walter, Philippe. *Canicule: Essai de mythologie sur "Yvain" de Chrétien de Troyes.* Paris: SEDES, 1988.

——. *La mémoire du temps: fêtes et calendriers de Chrétien de Troyes à La Mort Artu.* Paris: Champion, 1989.

——. *Christian Mythology.* Rochester, Vt.: Inner Traditions, 2014.

Warnerius of Basel. *Synodicus.* Edited by Johann Huemer in *Romanische Forschungen* 3 (1888): 319–30.

Index